WRITING TO SELL

Revised Edition

WRITING TO SELL

by SCOTT MEREDITH

HARPER & ROW, PUBLISHERS

NEW YORK AND EVANSTON

PN
147
.M48
1960

TO HELEN, *of course*

CONTENTS

vii

sionals' scripts and new writers' scripts — Why some editors *must* reject incorrectly prepared manuscripts — Should you quote a price for the manuscript? — Should you secure copyright and list copyright notice? — What about handwritten manuscripts? — Should you use a cover page? — Best tools for the writer — Sample first and subsequent pages — Should you mail scripts flat or folded? — The proper way to determine word count.

What *not* to write if you want to sell — The "why" of taboos: how they're born — General taboos in force at every market — Specific taboos of different markets — Permanent and temporary taboos — The triteness taboo, and how to tell if you've got one — Characters and situations to be avoided — The disgusting taboo — The bad-taste taboo — The advertisers and taboos — Trends in taboos — When can taboos be violated?

TWO: THE STORY-PLANNING AND PLOTTING FACTS

How to get ideas for stories — How to make them come in a steady stream — What about plots from real life and personal experience? — What personal experience really means — Should you write only about things you know? — Pulling ideas out of your mind — How about plotting devices and gadgets? — *Your* kind of idea — Ideas which come when you don't need them — Plotting without a compass: the who-knows-where-it's-going approach — Should you use a notebook?

The basic pattern underlying all successful fiction — Why fairy tales and classics and current magazine stories

are built from the same bricks — How to find the pattern
— Its importance — The vital difference between a plot
pattern and a formula — Elements of the basic plot pattern — How the elements work together — Analysis of each
ingredient of the basic plot pattern — Why your story must
contain all the elements.

acceptable motivation — The yardstick readers use on fiction motivation.

THREE: THE WRITING FACTS

FOUR: THE FINISHED-PRODUCT FACTS

story? — Which rights do magazines usually buy? — Will the publisher later release some of the rights he's bought? — Stories sold under pen names — First and second serial rights — Book rights and reprint book rights — Motion-picture rights, television rights, and radio rights — Foreign rights — Condensation rights — Selling rights by countries — When to consult an attorney — The attorney who isn't a publishing specialist.

INTRODUCTION

In January of 1951, which in a sense was a lifetime ago, another lifetime, I wrote a letter in answer to a blind ad which appeared in the Sunday *New York Times*. I was, at the time, selling lobsters by telephone for a company on Seventy-second Street and Columbus Avenue. I had quit teaching high-school English several months before and had exhausted every book and magazine house in the city searching for editorial work before accepting the job of peddling crustaceans by phone. My job was hardly uplifting. It consisted of calling a list of restaurants in New York and saying, parrotlike, "Good morning, would you like a quote on some nice fresh Maine lobsters today?" I sold a great many barrels of lobsters which were undoubtedly devoured in restaurants I had never entered. Had I kept at this line of work, I might well have become the lobster king of the Western world. But, you see, I wanted to be a writer. And it seemed to me in my youth that the quickest way to become a writer was to become an editor first.

The advertisement in the *Times* was asking for an editor familiar with the book and magazine field. I felt I qualified for the job because I had received countless rejection slips from the publishing world. And if I didn't quite know what kind of material they were buying in that winter of 1951, I certainly was an expert on what they were *not* buying. Well, on a particularly bleak Wednesday, after I'd sold my fourth barrel of lobsters for the day (the Chinese girl who sat at the desk opposite me and who specialized in dealings with the Chinese restaurants had sold five that day, I remember) and while I was sitting at my desk wondering what was happening up at *The Saturday Evening Post,* my wife called. The conversation went something like this:

ANITA: Hello, how's the lobster business today?
EVAN: Fine. We're selling them like shrimp patties.
ANITA: I just got a call from someone in reply to one of the letters you sent out. Can you talk?
EVAN: (With a surreptitious glance at his boss, the then lobster king of the Western world) Yes, go ahead.
ANITA: You're to go to 580 Fifth Avenue at 12:30 for a test of some sort.
EVAN: A test? What kind of a test?
ANITA: For an editorial position. Can you be there at 12:30?
EVAN: Sure, I can.
ANITA: Will you let me know how it turns out?
EVAN: I'll call as soon as I leave.
ANITA: Good luck.

I sat at my desk and dreamed of editorial nirvana. Ah, to work for a magazine, to learn the writing profession from the inside out. Anxiously, I ticked off the minutes to twelve noon. Then I bid a hasty good-by in Chinese to my co-worker and caught the subway to Times Square, shuttled to Grand Central and ran the distance to Forty-seventh and Fifth.

On the door was the legend:

SCOTT MEREDITH, INC.
Authors' Representatives

I almost did not enter. With my hand on the doorknob, I told myself this was not what I was looking for, I wanted an introduction to the *real* world of publishing, and besides who wanted to take a stupid old test when I should have been in the Automat eating my lunch? Well, apparently *I* wanted to take a stupid old test because I turned the knob and was greeted by a statuesque blonde receptionist who led me to a typewriter, handed me a manuscript, and said, "Please read this story and then write a report telling why you think it is either salable or unsalable. You have one hour." She was off and away before I could thank her, and I sat down to read the story and to write my report on it. The typewriter ribbon had apparently been torn in one spot by a previous test-taker and each time I came to that spot the carriage jammed. By the time I finished writing my report—I wrote eight pages, as I recall—I was angry enough to hurl that machine out the window. I didn't. I cornered the blonde instead and asked her what this was all about and she answered with a variation of "Don't call us; we'll call you," and away I went. I invested ten cents in a phone call to Anita, who seemed as disappointed by the entire encounter as I was. And I went back to selling lobsters.

The next day, I received a call from the agency. I was informed that a Mr. Marlowe would like to interview me and could I be there in a half hour? Throwing all caution to the winds, I told the lobster king of the Western world that I had to dash out of the office on something important, and I raced my way to Forty-seventh and Fifth, where I was interviewed by a man named Marlowe, who told me frankly that it was an absolute agency rule not to hire anyone without previous editorial experience. But, he said, the firm had been impressed with my letter and further impressed with my report on the story, and they were willing to bend that rule this one time and hire me. I would be hired, Mr. Marlowe explained, as a trainee and developed to a point where, ultimately, I would be his replacement. At first I glowed at this good news. Then, very shrewdly, and suspecting something fishy in this barrel of lobsters, I subtly asked, "And why are *you* leaving the job, Mr. Marlowe?"

Mr. Marlowe answered, "Because the agency has been selling so many of my own stories, it would be unprofitable for me to stay on here as a staff editor."

My ears perked up, my eyes sparked, I mumbled something incoherent, I grasped Mr. Marlowe's hand, I kissed his feet, and I took the job. Mr. Marlowe, I later discovered, was Mr. Stephen Marlowe, the mystery writer and creator of Chester Drum, private-eye. He did go on to free-lancing as a Meredith client, but not before he had completely familiarized me with the workings of the agency and passed on my more arduous training to Scott Meredith himself.

It was Steve Marlowe who introduced me to *Writing to Sell.* He brought the book out to me one February day and explained that a great deal of the agency's attitude toward writing and writers could be found in its pages, and that I might do well to study it as an introduction to the new job. I thanked him and Mr. Meredith for sending the book my way, and then went home with it, somewhat cynically prepared for the absorption of some "household hints" on how to write.

The book, to me, was a revelation. I had majored in English in college and read a dozen or more manuals on writing. I had taken all the creative writing courses (The Short Story, The Play, Poetry, Essays and Criticism) and I had been submitting my material regularly to magazines all over the country, and I had never made a sale. I never knew why I hadn't made a sale until I read Scott's book. (I beg the right to call him by his first name even though such familiarity is out of chronological order. But I have known Scott since that February in 1951, and when I finally left the agency to free-lance in May of 1953, I left with Scott's blessings and good wishes. He has been my agent and my friend for almost nine years. He sold my first story for $12.60, and my latest novel for close to a half-million dollars, and we have been fighting the literary battle together for a good long time now. So please forgive the anachronism.)

Writing to Sell, Scott had called his book, and the title was appropriate and just. This was no dry text explaining story in terms of outmoded techniques. This was no manual of boredom. It read like a fast-paced novel and there was information on every page, information which I eagerly digested and then redigested, information which I'd been longing to have from the first time I'd tried putting words on paper. With an enormous sense of innocent misdirection, I recalled one college instructor who had advised me and a classful of embryo writers to be "sure to type the words 'First North American Serial Rights Only' in the corner of any manuscript submitted to a magazine." Did she know she was hopelessly stamping the submission as amateurish? Here, for the first time, I found in Scott's book a purely professional approach to the business of writing. For say what one will, the *art* of writing is a vague term which produces images of winged muses flitting in the air over the author's head. When translated from the English, the *art* of writing becomes the *craft* of writing. And the craft of writing involves more than simply being able to spill one's guts onto the keys of a typewriter. It involves more than being able to string words into a glittering necklace. Or being able to describe beautifully the ocean on a misty day. Or even being able to penetrate deeply into the secret heart of a character. These are all a part of the craft of writing, but these qualities alone will not sell stories.

I cannot conceive of any writer, no matter how artistic his claims, who would be content to write with the knowledge that his manuscripts will be placed in the bottom drawer of his desk where, if he's lucky, his mother will one day find and read them. The art of writing is the craft of writing; and the craft of writing becomes and remains the *business* of writing. Writers write to be read. And the way to get stories or books read in this our twentieth century is to *sell* them to magazine or book publishers.

Scott Meredith's book contains no magic formulas; there *are* none when it comes to writing and selling. Nor does it purport to contain a packet of that mystical dust which, when sprinkled over any given manuscript, will transform it into a dazzling masterpiece. And yet, originally published in 1950, revised and brought up to date in this new edition, *Writing to Sell* has sold more copies than any other writing book I know in publishing history—and with good reason. It is a book written by a man who has himself been writer, editor and now literary agent. It is a book written by a man who knows the publishing field intimately and who is articulate enough to translate his everyday commerce into information which becomes meaningful to all writers, beginners or professionals. It is a book which cuts to the marrow of writing, which peels off the veneer of glamour and the pretentiousness of "serious art."

The talent is in the writer and will always be there and no book in the world will flame it into life where it does not exist. But this book provides a springboard into literary waters which can seem so damn dark and forbidding to the uninitiated. It does so in a style which is at once readable and entertaining. In fact, I warrant it will be read through the first time for the sheer pleasure of enjoying it. And after that, as I have done, the reader will return to it time and time again for the valuable information in its pages, until it becomes as necessary to his desk as the English dictionary.

EVAN HUNTER

The author wishes to thank *Writer's Digest* for permission to reprint his article "Can We Still Be Friends?" as part of the chapter on marketing and agents. He is also grateful to his brother, Sidney Meredith, for valuable assistance in many ways, and to the members of his staff, who suggested some of the chapter titles.

ONE: THE BUSINESS FACTS

1

YOU, WRITER: *Your place in the writing business*

I am not, generally speaking, a betting man, but I am willing to wager a modest sum that there are, among those of you who have bought this book and are now reading these opening lines, a number who have been plagued with a feeling of worried perplexity ever since you plunked down the necessary amount on the bookstore counter. You've heard somewhere that writing ability is something with which you're born, like blue eyes or a tip-tilted nose, and you're wondering whether or not trying to achieve literary success through study is a waste of money which might otherwise be spent on beer or ice-cream sodas.

You'd be absolutely right, and I'd even go down with you and help you talk the clerk into returning your money, if writing ability were the only requirement necessary in the building of a successful literary career. Basic writing ability is a product of many things such as heredity, childhood reading, and personality, and neither this book nor any other can affect the question of is-you-is-or-is-you-ain't-a-born-writer. But writing ability is not the only requirement, not by a thousand miles.

To have basic writing ability and no technical knowledge, and to try to earn a living writing stories, is equivalent to finding yourself suddenly endowed with a large amount of steel, lumber, and bricks, and, without any knowledge of architecture or building, setting out to earn your living building and selling houses. You might, by a fluke or by carefully examining houses which are already built, complete some which are approximately like professionally built houses, and even sell a few, but it is extremely unlikely that you will achieve any sort of major or lasting success at your work.

In the writing business, of course, there are a number of established authors who know nothing whatever about technique, and nevertheless manage to sell stories and go on selling them. Aside from the fact that these authors turn up about as often as quadruplets, which would make it downright silly for a new author to ignore technical study in the hope that he'll have the same kind of luck, it is interesting to note that these authors use, unconsciously, the same techniques that others with know-how use consciously. The psychological mystery of how these writers got this sense of structure isn't pertinent; the important thing is that there are definite methods in all ficion writing, and you need them.

Let's assume, then, for the sake of getting some genuine good out of this book, that you do have basic writing ability, that you are a born writer. The chances are, anyway, if you've gone to the trouble of buying or borrowing this book, and intend to keep plugging away at writing no matter what I have to say in it, that the assumption is correct: because I've found again and again that the surest indication of the genuine writer is that amount of push and drive inside him which keeps him struggling to succeed at writing. His early stories may not show it, and you sometimes have the feeling that the kindest thing would be to buy him a course in candymaking or welding, but, if he keeps working away at it, you have the pleasure of watching his stories change from terrible to fair to good to excellent.

With the basic ability behind you, and the drive to keep at it, you probably want to know what other ingredients, aside from technical knowledge, you'll need to succeed. What, for instance, about education and cultural background?

The best way to discuss the former, I think, is to consider the two best-known and most successful writers I represent, both of whom receive $5,000 or over per short story, and $50,000 and up per serial. One of them is a Harvard graduate; he holds a Phi Beta Kappa key and an M.A. degree. The other got as far as the eighth grade when his father passed away, and he has had to work for a living ever since.

Go down any list of successful writers, and you'll find that the lists of the educated and the not-so-educated are about equal in number. Personally, I don't believe that formal education or the lack of it makes a bit of difference either way. The important thing is that your education must be a good one, whether you've got a diploma to prove it or whether you've picked up your education through reading books or friendship with intelligent, knowledgeable people.

In other words, you've got to be able to think and write clearly; you've got to have a reasonable familiarity with the English language, so that you can use the right words at the right times and achieve the effects you desire; you've got to know how to use your eyes and be reasonably observant of the things around you, because the darnedest objects, people, and occurrences pop up in your stories and have to be described. It helps, of course, to be able to spell moderately well, and know how to use correct grammar, though even these aren't terribly important. Many successful writers I know are worse spellers and grammarians than some of the kids I met back in the fourth grade; but they turn out first-class stories and their wives retype them and correct the errors.

The same, of course, applies to cultural background—whatever that may be—and travel experience: a great many writers eat lamb chops with their hands, are unable to swoon over a Picasso however hard they try, and have traveled as far as two or three hundred miles in their lives.

The important reason which led to the fable that writers must be cultured and well traveled, of course, lies in the fact that you must know something about people and places if you're going to write about them. If, however, as seems to be the case with most people who want to write, you're sensitive and perceptive about human relations, and learn a great deal through local observation and reading, there's no reason in the world to wait until you're sixty and understand Life, or to spend ten years roughing it along the Upper Zambesi. Too often, the would-be writer's alleged wait for culture or "understanding" before he attacks the typewriter is a subconscious excuse for failure.

The question of what you're going to write, now that we've made another assumption and decided that you have the necessary background along with your basic ability, is one which can be answered by asking yourself another question, and a very simple one: What do you like to read?

There used to be a very popular theory, now steadily lessening in popularity because it has been proven incorrect over and over again, that the writing business should be conducted along the lines of a standard school system. You start with the kindergarten, the lowest-payment and lowest-prestige field, usually the pulp magazines (the all-fiction magazines, called pulps because of the rough pulp paper on which they are printed), and, after gaining experience, gradually work your way up to the highest level, generally the slick magazines (the mass-circulation, general magazines, called slicks because of the slick, smooth paper on which they are printed), or the quality magazines (the intellectual magazines which run quality, arty, and experimental fiction).

This theory, which sounds perfectly logical until you examine it closely, fails because of one obvious fact: no man can do his best work at a job he dislikes. And in the writing business, you've always got to do your best work, because the competition, even in the lowest-paying fields, is tremendous.

In other words, a man whose favorite type of story, such as mystery fiction, appears both in the pulps and slicks *may* start in the pulps and gain experience before moving into the slicks, but a man whose favorite kind of story is a strictly slick type—such as the serious family-problem story, for which there is no pulp counterpart—can only harm himself and delay his success by forcing himself to write, for example, science-fiction for the pulps.

Many top-level writers started in the pulp kindergarten: to name just a few, P. G. Wodehouse, Agatha Christie, C. S. Forester, MacKinlay Kantor, and Luke Short. The basic difference in their career plans, though they rose in the indicated manner, is that they *liked* the pulp magazines and the kind of stories published in the pulp magazines, at least at the time they were writing them. And though they've changed the type of publications in which they appear, most of them are still writing the same kinds of stories.

The same is certainly true at the present time. In the past year, perhaps twenty writers for lesser fields among my clients made first slick sales, some of them repeating so steadily that they will soon be moving entirely out of the lesser fields into the slicks. Nearly all of them, however, will be writing the same kinds of stories they wrote for the secondaries: they're going into the slicks entirely because of the greater payment and prestige, and because of the greater opportunities for *additional* income (for example, more stories are bought for adaptation for television from the slicks than from any other field).

In choosing *your* kind of writing, forget for the moment that there are different kinds of magazines, like pulps, slicks, and qualities: for I'm going to show you in future chapters, anyway, that pulp and slick and quality stories are not so different from each other in content as you might think. (I'm also going to show you in the next chapter, incidentally, that only one of these fields—the slicks—is worth a permanent stay.) But forget this for the moment, and concentrate on the kind of story you most like to read and would most enjoy writing.

You've got to be absolutely honest with yourself here. This does not mean the kind of story you'd like to tell your friends you're writing, or the kind of story at which your friends won't sneer: it means the kind of story you most like to read and write.

If you receive genuine enjoyment from the very literary, experimental, offbeat kind of story published by one of the quality quarterlies—and remember what I said about being honest with yourself: I am not referring to enjoyment of the awe in people's faces when you carry a quality magazine around, with the cover facing outward—then that is the only kind of story for you to write (though not necessarily, as I'll explain, with a view toward selling it to a quality magazine). If you really enjoy the light love or family-problem stories as featured in the slicks, then the light love or family-problem story should be your specialty. And if you get the most pleasure out of mystery fiction, then specialize in mystery fiction—though, again, not necessarily for the crime-fiction pulp magazine.

I've stressed the matter of selection of a type and specialization in that type because it is an important step which should be taken as early as possible in your career. The writer who does one kind of story one day, another type the following day, and a third type the day after that will never become particularly proficient in any of them; and, furthermore, his scattered and varied appearances will never build for him a strong following, because most readers prefer a single type of story above all other types and give their allegiance to writers who constantly supply them with that type. Think about the most successful writers of our time, and you'll find that, almost without exception, all of them specialize and write one type of story. Choose your type, therefore, and, though there's no harm in taking an occasional busman's holiday if another type of story enters your mind and howls to be written, stay with that chosen type most of the time.

I should mention, incidentally, that, if you choose a type which sells both to the pulps and slicks, and decide to gain experience first in the pulps, don't make the error of assuming that you may write badly or must write down. A quick look at some of the better current pulp magazines will dispel this notion: some amazingly good writing appears in the pulps today, which is why agents are occasionally able to take stories clients had planned for the pulps at $100 and sell them to the slicks at $1,000. Let me say it once again: you've got to write your best whichever type of story you choose, which is why you must choose a type to which you *can* give your best. The writer who pounds out a story carelessly, telling himself, "What the hell—it's awful but it's only for the pulps," will find that the pulps have a large supply of rejection slips, with one set aside for him.

If you start in a lesser field such as the pulps, by the way, and begin to succeed in it, you'll find that, despite any uneasy expectations you may have had, your relatives and friends won't sneer at you. No, pulp writers and other writers for lesser fields are sneered at in generalizations, rarely face to face. There is something so impressive about the receipt of a check for a story, and the subsequent publication of that story, that the man who has sneered at the pulps for years as trash will stumble all over himself to get to know you better if you have a check for a pulp sale in your pocket, or a copy of a pulp magazine containing your story.

Once you've chosen your specialty, you'll want to decide whether you're going to sign your stories with your own name or a pen name, for your by-line is your trademark and a valuable property, and should be retained and built up with each story you sell. Generally, I advise new writers against the use of a pseudonym, and here's why:

There are several valid reasons that professional writers use pen names. For one thing, a man's name doesn't always fit the type of fiction he writes: a writer of rough, tough, side-of-mouth detective stories may be unwilling to have them appear under his real name, if his real name is Percy Harmondyne Whistlewillow. Women who write male-category stories hide their sex under pen names; for example, B. M. Bower, Eli Colter, and Stewart Toland, all writers of Westerns and all women. Some very prolific writers use pseudonyms in addition to their own names because they frequently have several stories appearing in single issues of magazines, and editors don't favor repeated by-lines on the grounds that it looks as though the writer owns stock in the magazine. In a recent issue of one of America's top slick magazines, three of the stories were by a single author.

Another reason may be that the author's name is foreign and unpronounceable and it is to his advantage to adopt a pleasant-sounding name which will be more easily remembered. An example is Joseph Conrad, whose real name was Teodor Józef Konrad Korzeniowski. Still another reason may be that the author is writing about a subject which may get him in personal trouble, such as a story we recently sold which dealt with crooked gambling. Its author, a resident of the city in which the story was laid, hid under a pseudonym because he might get his head kicked in if his identity were known. And one more is that a man may be writing part-time until he sells steadily and becomes better established, and his job would be endangered if the boss found out he wasn't devoting his full faculties day and night to the sale of more and more knitted ties.

All of these reasons are sound enough, but they are not the reasons most new writers adopt pseudonyms. These are two-fold: "because people would kid me if they knew that I write" and "because I expect to improve as I go along and I don't want my early efforts to be held against me."

We've already, I think, disposed pretty thoroughly of the first reason. People may sneer at lesser-field writers in the abstract, and people may grin at poor old Joe who thinks he can write stories, but the sneers stop and the grins vanish when the stories sell. And since your by-line, whether pseudonym or real, would come before the public eye only in the event of sale, it's muddy thinking to use a pseudonym for that reason.

The same principle applies to the second. A skill is bound to improve as you keep plugging away at it, whether the skill is writing or knitting or whistling through your teeth, and, except in extremely rare cases of retrogression caused by such things as an increasing love for the contents of a whisky bottle, most successful writers' first efforts don't compare to their later ones. You may be sure your early efforts won't be held against you. Quite the contrary, as a matter of fact: your audience will like you better and better as they watch your stories grow better and better.

If you have a valid reason for using a pen name, use one by all means. But don't use a pseudonym on the grounds of mistaken reticence or because you like to think of people wondering Who-Is-the-Mysterious-Figure-Lurking-Behind-the-Name-of-Herman-Blugg? All you'll get out of *that*, as a top-selling novelist groaned to me recently, is the frustrating experience of listening to your wife explain to people, who are unaware that you write under a pen name, why you stay at home all day like a bum instead of going out to work like decent people.

Make your choice intelligently but make it. The sooner you begin to build up your name, the sooner your name will mean more dollars per manuscript.

This book is a work on writing to sell, and my comments in this chapter have been concerned, as will all my comments in the chapters which follow, with commercial writing and placement for payment. It must be stressed, however, that these principles apply every bit as much to the work of so-called "serious" writers who feel they are less concerned with writing for money than with contributing important material to the stockpile of the world's great literature.

The one thing the serious writer most often forgets, and which he should remember above everything else, is that almost no man on earth has ever succeeded in setting out deliberately to create a classic or masterpiece. Shakespeare, Zola, Dickens, Twain, and almost every other writer whose work has survived for beyond his own generation, wrote—though without sacrificing his own literary values—entirely with the view of pleasing the current public and making money at it. Aside from the natural inner hope which every writer feels every time he writes a story, there was no deliberate, calculated attempt to create a centuries-surviving classic. They merely wrote the best manuscript possible and, because of the high quality of their work, and because they achieved enormous fame and popularity which was remembered past their generation, their stories and plays became classics and are still enjoyed today.

A very few writers were unpopular in their own time and achieved a certain amount of attention afterward, but their later fame has been, generally, critical rather than popular. Shakespearean play productions are still sellouts today, and Dickens and Zola and Twain are still read and enjoyed by millions, but few of the critical-fame boys are much read outside of required school study.

By this token, perhaps surprisingly, a writer today has a better chance of creating a classic and achieving a lasting position in the literary Hall of Fame by writing for the popular magazines, because of the vast audiences, than by writing ultraliterary, you-interpret-it-for-yourself material for the little experimental magazines, where the audiences are tiny, composed of feuding factions in which each man believes the other fellow's idea of the Good Literature is all wrong, and where—even there—only one-tenth of the audience will understand the story the way the author intended it.

2

OFF ON THE RIGHT FOOT: *The intelligent approach to the markets*

What I have begun to do, in the preceding chapter, is nudge you gently toward the slicks as your best permanent base of operations. In this chapter, the nudge becomes a shove.

You'll see why as we examine each field and compare the advantages or disadvantages of each. In every way, and from every angle, the advantages in the slicks outweigh the others by a ton.

Let's start with the pulps.

The pulp magazines were launched, most of them around the turn of the century, as male-interest counterparts of the slick magazines of the period. Like the slicks, they published stories in a variety of categories: the major difference being that slick magazines were planned to be read by the entire family and pulps were slanted for male readers only. The pulps were immediately successful on the newsstands of the country and the variety pulps were soon joined by dozens, and then scores, of pulp magazines, each devoting its entire contents to a *single* type of story: detective-story magazines, Westerns, sports-story magazines, love-story magazines, Western-romance magazines (featuring love stories in a Western setting), aviation or air-war-story magazines, jungle-story magazines, fantasy magazines (featuring stories dealing with purely imaginative subjects such as vampires, werewolves, and the like), horror-terror magazines (containing crime stories stressing sadism, torture, beatings), and science-fiction magazines (featuring stories of the future generally based on a sound scientific concept and going on from there).

In those days, a good price for a first slick sale was around two hundred dollars, and the pulps, many of which paid around five cents a word, trailed not too far behind.

In more recent years, however, two major changes have taken place in the pulp field. One is that the variety pulps have vanished entirely and the single-category pulps have shrunk in number from an army to the remnants of a platoon, killed off one by one by lack of newsstand space (wholesalers and distributors today just don't want to bother with a *lot* of magazines with circulations of around a hundred thousand each; they prefer to concentrate on fewer, multimillion-circulation magazines) and by the arrival of television with all that free drama and the paperbacks with all those inexpensive novels. As a result, many of the pulp categories mentioned above, once containing a dozen or more magazines each, no longer exist at all; other types have just four or five magazines at most. In the heyday of the pulps, there were over two hundred all-fiction magazines on the stands. Today there are perhaps one-tenth that number. The other major change is that, as slick-story prices have zoomed upward, pulp prices have zoomed in the opposite direction.

The average starting payment in the pulps today is one cent a word, with gradual improvement—raises at a half cent to a cent a word as you keep selling—to a current maximum in the field of about four cents a word. There is also a magazine or two in the field which starts at a cent and never goes higher than *two* cents; there is also a magazine or two which starts at a cent and never goes higher at all, paying that fixed rate for all its material; and there are even a couple of magazines which start new writers at one-*half* cent a word and advance in quarter-cent leaps to their top of a cent per word.

Here, obviously, is the chief disadvantage of the pulp field: the fact that you can't hope to start at much better than $50 per average-length, 5,000-word short story, or end at much better than a couple of hundred dollars for a story of the same length. Novelettes, which run as high as 20,000 words in the pulps, bring more money, of course, but, as in all fiction fields, only a limited number in this length are used compared to shorts, and a few of the pulps use no novelettes at all—preferring instead to buy only very short scripts and thereby give their contents pages a loaded-with-material appearance. That is why you can count the $10,000-a-year men in the pulps today on the fingers of one hand, and many pulp Big Names find at the end of the year that their earnings have been on a par with that of a union busboy—$70 or $80 per week.

The chief advantage in the pulps stems from this disadvantage, naturally. Because the payment today is so much lower than that of the slicks, the purchase standards are somewhat lower too (though not, as I've warned, so much lower than you'll get anywhere if you try writing *down* to the pulps). And because, as I've pointed out, your stuff is bound to get better as you keep doing it, those of you who have chosen a type of story which sells both to the pulps and the slicks are lucky. If your stuff is not of slick quality at the moment, you can earn while you learn by selling to the pulps until your stuff reaches the point of development where it begins to sell to the slicks.

The development or movement of the quality of pulp writing throughout the history of the field might be described as V-shaped. In the early, highest-paying period of the pulps, the quality was at an extremely high level, and it isn't surprising that the names you see in very old copies of pulp magazines are among the greatest names in modern literature today. During the nineteen thirties, forties, and early fifties, pulp quality took a nose dive along with its prices, and it was during this period that the field earned its reputation as trash. And currently, the quality of writing in the pulps, particularly the better ones, is again—though unlike the payment prices—surprisingly high.

It isn't, self-evidently, quite as high as the quality of writing in the slicks, but the margin of difference between pulp and slick quality—say, for example, in a pulp or slick crime story—grows steadily smaller. I refer you to comparative reading of pulp and slick stories in one category, an experience which may surprise you. Therefore, by writing pulps at the start, you can do your style or ability no harm. Rather, you'll be polishing and sharpening it by repeated use right into the Big Time.

In short, the pulps are a wonderful experience field, to be thoroughly recommended to all writers whose story choice fits pulps and whose stuff requires additional grooming before they can go to the Grand Ball. It should, however, be considered a temporary stopover, where you can remain only as long as necessary.

The major difference between stories appearing in the quality magazines and those in the other two fields is that nearly all pulp stories are designed only to entertain, and many slick stories are designed only to entertain, but quality stories have a purpose in addition to entertainment—the focus of a strong spotlight on a problem of mankind or a basic problem of everyday living, such as antiminority prejudice, economic conditions among the sharecroppers, or a man's discovery that he no longer loves his family. Most quality stories attempt, by giving a single example of a problem, to illustrate and probe into the problem as it exists generally. A good example is *The*

Ox-Bow Incident, which, by telling the story of one group of men who were lynched and then discovered to have been innocent, illustrates the wrongness of lynch law under *any* circumstances.

For quite a long time, this sort of theme was an absolute monopoly within the quality field. You could never sell a story concerned, for example, with rape, or extramarital relations, or mistreatment of Puerto Ricans to the slicks or pulps, which would never take the chance of playing with dynamite; therefore, if you wanted to write a story along one of these lines, it had to be done for the quality magazines. The same applied, generally speaking, to experimental handling of any kind: a story off the accepted and well-traveled trail could rarely be sold to any field other than the quality field.

This line of demarcation has faded until it is now almost invisible, particularly as far as the slicks are concerned. More and more, the slicks are publishing any kind of story with any kind of theme as long as the editors believe it to be a good theme and a good story. Touchy themes, such as racial or sexual problems, it is true, are still regarded by the slicks with a great deal of awe, and they will still hail as extra-special a story which the quality magazines would accept as normal fare, but they're moving surely and steadily in the right direction—the direction of wide-open, unrestricted buying. And, more and more, the emigration from the qualities to the slicks is becoming as steady as from the pulps.

As in the pulps, the reasons are twofold: economics and opportunity. The quality field is, and has nearly always been, a comparatively limited one. There are very few quality magazines and nearly all of them publish far more critical, political, and analytical articles than they do fiction. An average of two fiction pieces as opposed to ten articles per issue extends throughout the field. Add to this the fact that several of the quality magazines have strong favorites among authors and run a tight little group over and over again, with the addition of a newcomer an extremely rare event.

The circulations and, therefore, the advertising earnings of most of the quality magazines are comparatively limited, which makes the payment rate limited, too. The average payment for a short story sold to a quality magazine is $150, a mighty slim figure when you add the fact that, for the reasons given, you can't sell very many of them. Most quality writers today, as a result, contribute occasionally to the quality magazines, but sell the bulk of their output to the slicks, which buy exactly the same kinds of stories from them and pay many times as much. Typical examples are Jerome Weidman and Shirley Jackson.

If quality stories are your choice, the best advice is to go and do likewise.

The slick magazine field, it seems to me, offers three important reasons for qualifying as your best permanent base of operations:

1. Best payment
2. Best opportunities
3. Best springboard

The lowest price you will receive when you sell your first short story to a slick magazine is $750—this is the standard opener payment at most slick markets. Some will sometimes pay as high as $1,100 for a first purchase. These are bottom figures; the top is never set. A good many writers receive as high as $5,000 or $6,000 for 5,000-word stories; at least one has received as high as $10,000 for a story of this length.

Naturally, with prices like these, your competition is pretty stiff. In the pulps, for example, you are competing only with the best writers in the pulp field; in the slicks, you're competing with the best writers in the world. Top slick magazines receive several hundred submissions daily, some of them more than a hundred thousand yearly, and buy a comparatively tiny fraction. Obviously, it is sometimes a long, hard fight to break in, but, just as obviously, it's worth it.

It has become, as a matter of fact, just a trifle easier in recent years because of the gradual decline of the Big Name system. At one time, almost every name on the contents page of a slick magazine was recognizable as a famous literary figure, and the appearance of a new name was quite a novelty. Today, Big Names are still used, but not quite so much to the exclusion of all others. Magazines realize, as ever, that the appearance of world-famous names on their covers and contents pages will sell more copies because of the enormous following these writers have built up, but they also realize that more audience must be given to the fresh new talents who will be the Big Names of tomorrow.

In the past two years, for example, more slick stories by new writers have been bought than in any equal period of time in this century. Almost every issue of the slick magazines today contains one or two stories by new writers, and several issues recently have contained only new writers' stories. The era of Big Names Only still isn't over by any means, and—as in the example given in the last chapter—editors will still lapse occasionally and come to depend so much on one writer that they use several of his stories in one issue, but opportunities for the new writer in the slicks have widened immeasurably.

Certainly it is far easier to sell a story to a lesser field, such as the pulps, than it is to sell a story to the slicks; it is even far easier to crack the pulps and sell ten stories in a row than to make a first sale to the slicks. One simple fact you've got to remember, however, is that a single slick sale at the base rate of $750 is equivalent to the sale of *fifteen* 5,000-word stories to a lesser field at one cent a word, and that a prominent slick writer's sale of a short story at $5,000 is equivalent to the sale of *one hundred* to a lesser field.

Another important point is that, far more than any other field, the receipt of money for the sale of a story to the slicks usually means more money. When you've made a sale in another field, that's it; you've collected, ninety-nine times out of a hundred, all the money you're going to collect. With a slick story, however, the initial sale is frequently only the beginning. There are then foreign, radio, television, motion picture, and other rights to be considered.

Possibly because they still think of pulp stories as they used to be, and aren't overly familiar with other fields, few other-rights buyers will purchase anything but slick stories. It is rare that a pulp story will sell anywhere beyond the initial buyer, but slick stories usually draw subsequent British sale, plus others like French, South American, Australian, Scandinavian, and Italian. One story we've handled has sold fourteen different foreign rights thus far, earning through translations alone (in other words, exclusive of such things as movie sale) somewhat more than the high original purchase price all over again. Ninety per cent of the magazine stories bought for television come from slick magazines; 95 percent of the magazine stories bought for the movies come from slick magazines. Payment for the right to adapt a published magazine story for television generally averages about a thousand dollars; payment for the purchase of a magazine story for the movies starts at that figure and can run as high as fifty thousand.

The same applies, as well, if you are thinking of starting out in the magazine field as a springboard and working your way into novel writing, or writing for the movies or television—or if you hope to write novels and/or do an occasional movie or television stint in addition to your magazine writing. All of these fields have produced considerable home-grown talent—writers who have never done any other type—but far and away the largest number of the top people have made their entry through the magazine field.

Most magazine writers eventually do books as well. For one thing, a writer with an established magazine reputation can generally sell a book manuscript relatively easily, unlike the hellish job involved when a novel is the first thing you've written. For another thing, magazine writing is excellent training for novel writing—which is why so many published novels, particularly paperbacks, are expansions and developments of scripts originally sold and published as magazine stories. And for a third, book publishers regularly invite good magazine writers to do novels for their lists. Motion-picture and television companies do the same sort of scouting: a writer who has begun to build up a name in the magazines will often receive an invitation to write for television or pictures. And if a writer is especially anxious to do movie or television work, and an invitation isn't forthcoming, his agent can generally arrange a deal which puts him to work on the screenplay or teleplay of one of his own stories purchased for filming or televising.

There are three other fields which merit discussion in this chapter, since they also contain a fair number of markets each. These are the confessions, the juveniles, and the sophisticated men's magazines.

The confessions, though generally published on smooth paper, are not properly part of the slick-magazine field, since they publish a single kind of story rather than a variety of types: a love or marriage story with a confession-of-wrongdoing-or-error theme. These are supposed to be authentic real-life experiences of the writers, and sometimes confession magazines request an affidavit certifying that the story is true before they pay for it, even though all of them will buy an unlimited number of stories from a writer.

Generally, confession stories are written in the first person and from a woman's viewpoint, although the magazines occasionally buy third-person stories or stories told from a male viewpoint.

Perhaps the greatest objection to confessions as a choice of a permanent field is the fact that the very nature of the magazines makes the stories overly alike, and therefore somewhat restricting to the author.

The traditional course of the action in a confession story is a sin followed by suffering followed by penitence followed by happiness or the promise of happiness. It is based on a simple set of factors—since the magazine is devoted to confessions, the heroine must have sinned in order to have something to confess. Then, in order to secure the readers' sympathy, she must suffer for her sin, repent, and subsequently gain the happiness or promise of happiness which is due her as the result of her new understanding of right and wrong.

Some of the rules which once governed confession stories have now been relaxed. For a long time, for example, the sin—by editorial requirement—had to be sexual (usually premarital relations) in almost every story published; now sexual sin stories are used only occasionally, and the sin may be any kind of violation of moral behavior, such as cruelty to one's child or unreasoning jealousy of one's neighbor. Formerly, the sin had to be pretty much intentional, because the heroine was a bad girl who became good only after her suffering showed her that her way of life had been wrong; now her sin may be the result of her environment, or even innocent error (for example, where the heroine is not careful in choice of friends and gets into trouble through her association with them).

The basic concept of the confession story, however—the sin or wrong step followed by realization of its wrongness, followed by subsequent happiness or hope for happiness—cannot be changed, and the result is a basic similarity of story which most authors find they cannot continue to do for very long. Other types have the similarity-of-story trouble, too—in the detectives, for example, most stories start with a murder and end with capture of the murderer—but there is less restriction in the order of events in between.

And then, of course, there is the sad fact that, since confession stories are supposed to be true, they are always published sans by-line, and the author will never receive public credit or recognition for them.

For these reasons, the confessions are not a particularly good bet as a permanent field. The payment is rather good, however—three to six cents a word—and much of the writing and handling is almost on slick par, and some of the confessions have begun to run occasional non-confession, straight love stories. The field is well worth considering as a starter, therefore, to the writer who plans to write romantic or marriage-problem stories for the slicks, but doesn't feel his stuff is quite ready.

The juvenile field should be considered by the ambitious writer only as an opportunity for taste-of-blood, because it isn't too hard to crack and it can provide you fairly rapidly with the experience of earning money at writing.

It isn't so good, however, as a permanent field, or as a steppingstone to a higher field such as the slicks. The objection to permanency in the juveniles is economic, too, for the juvenile field is the lowest paying of all. With just a few exceptions, the average payment price is one quarter to one half cent a word; and, because you're writing for youngsters, the stories must be quite short. The average top length for children below ten is about a thousand words, for older children about three thousand. And you've got to sell a great many five- and ten-dollar stories to buy hamburgers and sirloin steak these days.

The trouble with the juveniles as a steppingstone is that, obviously, a story for children may—or must—be far simpler in plotting, language, and emotional relations between characters than an adult story. As a result, except for the inevitable smoothing out and improvement in your work which comes from any kind of writing, the idea of writing juveniles as training for adult fiction is like getting a job as a clerk in a pharmacy to train for a career as a doctor.

A few topnotch writers have come out of the juveniles, the best known being Clarence Budington Kelland, and a few writers make a good living in the juveniles by turning out tons of copy for the small-pay magazines and hitting the few better-pay magazines regularly. But all things considered, permanency or near permanency in the juvenile field is advisable only: (a) if you have an overwhelming desire to entertain children and place this before any other consideration, and (b) if you don't care much about money, or do care about money but have an independent income, such as a husband.

The sophisticated men's magazines, a relatively new field, have one basic and rigid requirement—sex and plenty of it— so they're not for you if you tend to blush easily. They are edited primarily for the young, sophisticated male of college age or just-barely-post-college age; they surround their prose content with photos and drawings of young ladies wearing little more than enigmatic smiles; and they require that fiction submitted to them be just as uninhibited.

There are students of magazine publishing in America who tend to compare today's sophisticated men's magazines with the sex-story pulps of the thirties, but the comparison really isn't appropriate because the old pulps were deadly serious in their approach to sex, making the concluding sex scene the entire point of the story and describing the sexual activity in as detailed a manner as the existing postal laws would permit. The present-day ribald magazines, however, take a far more lighthearted, humorous approach to the matter; their concern is as much with the quest as the conquest, as much with the pursuit as the prize. Their interest lies much more with stories of young men trying to succeed with the ladies, than with what happens once they do succeed.

The preferred locale here is the big city scene, Madison Avenue rather than Main Street, since the metropolis is the sophisticate's traditional stamping ground; historical or period fiction is rarely used, since modernity is the keyword; and, because lighthearted roguery is the slant, the serious results of some romances—such as pregnancy—are to be avoided. For that matter, the same applies to most serious aspects of life. A serious story is occasionally used, but the big emphasis is on fun and games.

Lengths in the sophisticated men's field are short—2,500 to 3,500 words are your best bets—and the big advantage in the field is that the pay is very good indeed. Some of the magazines start at $100 to $150 per script, but others go as high as $3,000 for a lead piece, which is why many really big names appear regularly in the major magazines in this field. The disadvantage is equally obvious; it's a pretty limited and restricted field in which the writer must work, and even sex can grow tiresome, at least on the printed page.

I hope that the preceding discussions on the advantages or disadvantages of each field have helped you pick yours, and that it is the slicks—for my experience has shown me that the slicks are the best bet as a permanent base. Even if you've chosen another, however, I hope that the decision is now firm and unyielding. The important thing is to make the decision and stick by it.

In many of the chapters which turn up later in the book, particularly those dealing with idea-getting and plotting and style, and other aspects of technique, I am going to show that, except for certain variations in handling, the basic facts and rules are the same whichever type of fiction you choose, or whichever field you select as a starter or for permanent stay—

detective stories, light love stories, quality stories, marriage-problem stories, juveniles, novels, plays, or what have you. It is essential, however, that you pick your type of story and field right at the start, so that your general technique may be curved and bent to meet specific requirements. And these choices, I trust, you have now made.

3

THE CURRENT SITUATION: *What editors buy*

The most popular-sized story in the New Writers set is the short-short, that brief little job running around fifteen hundred or two thousand words in length. This is too bad, because the short-short is about the worst length a new writer can choose.

It is easy to understand why the short-short is so attractive to newcomers. On the basis of its brevity, the short-short seems easier to write than the normal-length short story of five thousand words, because there are less words to get down and less blank pages to fill. It also seems easier to plot and plan, because a little story, logically, should require less complicated occurrences than a bigger story—particularly if the little story consists entirely of a build-up to a surprise ending.

Well, the short-short story is *not* the easiest to plot and write —not the kind of short-short which is salable in the current market, anyway. It is, perhaps, the hardest.

With the arrival of World War II, the steady decline of the traditional O. Henry or surprise-ending short-short story, where every event leads up to a final shock or twist, was accelerated more than ever. Popularity of the surprise-ending story in magazines had been fading for some time, because readers had been fed so many hundreds through the years that they were becoming a little bored with the form, particularly since they were now almost always able to predict the shocker or twist early in the stories. When the war added additional importance to the grip-the-reader element in fiction, the final nails were hammered into the surprise-ending story's coffin.

Men were enlisting and being inducted; members of almost every family were being shipped overseas to take part in some of the worst battles in human history. Readers, as a result, found themselves beset with terrible worries in addition to those of everyday living, and they just could not concentrate as well on stories which didn't grip them at once and hold their attention tightly right through to the end. Few surprise-ending short-shorts were able to do this, because the concentration was so heavy on the all-important ending that the build-up preceding it was usually rather routine and lacking in drama. The result was inevitable: surprise-ending short-shorts faded out of the picture, to be replaced by orthodox, full stories in miniature.

That is the short-short story today: a complete story, with all the important ingredients of a complete story, told in shorter length. No rule in this writing business is all-embracing, and you will still see an occasional very fresh surprise-ending short-short in the magazines, but the ratio has switched from nine hundred and ninety-five surprise-ending stories in each thousand published short-shorts to about five in each thousand. The public has found that the full-story-in-miniature short-short is more satisfying.

It's a mighty tough job to do, however, which is why so many short-shorts in magazines these days are by established rather than new writers. You'll discover, when you've worked at fiction writing for a while, that it will take a lot of writing of salable, normal-length short stories to make you skillful enough to do the same job in half or one-third the wordage.

Another reason most agents turn new writers away from short-shorts is that the short-short lessens the writer's selling odds at the stage of the game where he most needs the odds on his side. Some magazines don't use short-shorts at all and all magazines which do use them use a great many more normal-length short stories. As a result, you're shooting for a one-per-issue spot when you send a short-short to most magazines, whereas there are a half dozen openings per issue for a normal-length short story.

The same problem, incidentally, applies to the writing of novelettes (stories, generally speaking, in the eight to fifteen thousand word range); short novels (usually stories from twenty to twenty-five thousand words); or serials (forty to seventy thousand worders which run in installments) when you're breaking in. Some magazines don't use these lengths at all and most magazines which use them run only one or two per issue. There's an additional consideration too: the novelette, short novel, and serial are usually the stellar feature in the issue, given top billing on the cover and contents page, and the editor will usually prefer that they be done by Big Names—nationally famous authors, or authors who have appeared often enough in the magazine to have big followings among its readers.

Novelettes, short novels, and serials, of course, bring the biggest money in the magazine field, but you'd be wise to plan to start with shorts and, when you've begun to build up a reputation, work into the longer lengths.

When writing your shorts, by the way, keep away from oversized and off-length jobs; sixty-five hundred and seven thousand worders, for instance. Short stories frequently ran as high as these lengths some years ago, but the current trend is toward getting more pieces into each issue, which means shorter lengths for each piece. The preferred length currently is forty-five hundred to five thousand words. When your story goes above five thousand, it must sell *despite* its length, which means you've given it an added burden. We have, on occasion, sold very outsized short stories, but, since editors must balance the contents of their magazines and an outsized story may require reshuffling of the entire issue, the stories might not have sold if their quality had been a shade lower.

There used to be a time, not so very long ago, when you could not read a magazine without wading through a solid sea of Glamour. The magazine hero who did not own a yacht or two was practically *persona non grata*, and most magazine characters thought nothing of leaping nimbly from Park Avenue to Newport to Miami Beach to Monte Carlo. The stories, with very few exceptions, worked hard to be escapist; the everyday guy or gal in an everyday job could read them and momentarily escape into a moneyed world very different from the one he or she encountered in real life.

Today, along with the trend toward realism or near realism in all media of entertainment, the glamour-pusses are disappearing from the magazine pages. In their place has come the girl who works in the next office and the boy who lives around the corner, and the small or medium-sized "average" American town is replacing the Glittering Big City locale (except, as stated earlier, in the sophisticated men's magazines).

The purpose is greater reader-identification: stories, people, and places with which the readers can more readily identify themselves. Because the people in the stories are like the reader or like people he knows, because the settings and locales are like those the reader knows intimately, because the problems are like those the reader has encountered or could possibly encounter, the reader can more easily picture himself in those situations—and he is, as a result, in closer tune and sympathy with the stories. He can, conceivably, enjoy stories about millionaires or movie stars, which is why some are still run occasionally, but they're always, editors feel, a bit like fantasies to him; it is only when you parallel his own life that you begin to talk his language and get close to him.

Don't misunderstand this to mean that every story today

must be an exact reflection of the more mundane aspects of everyday life, with every hero concerned only with getting the boss to give him a five-buck raise. Few of us, for example, have actually experienced the sort of whirlaway she-loves-me-today-she-hates-me-tomorrow sort of courtship featured in most light love stories in the slicks. The important point is that when the hero courts the girl by taking her out on his three-hundred-foot yacht, we have to take the author's word for it; when the hero takes the heroine out rowing, we know just what he means.

This trend toward closer reader-identification exists as much in the pulps as it does in the slicks; it is, today, a characteristic of all fields. In the detective pulps, for example, the hero used to be a hard-drinking, blonde-chasing private eye, or a steely-eyed city dick; today, more and more, stories are favored which feature an average guy who suddenly finds himself in a murder jam, just as average guys have many times in real life, and fights his way out of it in his own human, untrained-to-handle-murder-situations manner, because he must do so to save his neck. Even Western heroes are no longer always fearless or dead shots. They're a little hardier than we are because they live in a locale where hardiness is a requirement of existence, but they miss when they try a too-difficult shot at the villain, and they sweat and feel the normal emotions of fear when the villain's bullet whizzes close past their ears.

Another aspect of this same trend is the fact that, generally, your stories should concern themselves with the doings of a hero and/or heroine in his or her twenties or early thirties, rather than with old people or children. There have been periods in which a great many old-people and children stories have been used, but editors have now come to feel that the reader-identification with people of those ages is inadequate: only a small portion of their audience is composed of old people or people young enough to remember clearly their childhood emotions or reactions. Again these rules are not absolute—we've sold some old-people and children stories this month, and will possibly continue to do so every month in the future—but the proportion of these stories purchased will continue to be tiny compared to those dealing with young adults. You understand, naturally, that I am referring to magazines of general circulation here, and not to juvenile magazines, which only purchase stories dealing with children, or to institutional magazines which circulate largely among aged people and frequently run stories concerning their problems.

Possibly because, under the logic of reader-identification, a man can have one big adventure in his lifetime but it becomes downright implausible when he has a couple of dozen, or possibly just because no really outstanding characters have turned up in recent years, editors aren't much interested in series characters. A few deliberately discourage it, turning down stories which deal with the same set of characters as those used in a previous story. Tugboat Annie, Jeeves, Scattergood Baines, and others, of course, continue to go on and on, and undoubtedly a few more can be launched, but you'd better wait until you've built up a big reputation first. Then you can use your huge reader following as a club when you tell the editor that you want to do a series about So-and-So, or else.

The reader-identification trend is an important one, and I suggest you make special note of it. Too many rejection slips are attached to good stories which miss this angle.

One May morning, I received a short story from a talented young writer, together with a note asking if I would be kind enough to rush it through to market at once. It was an Independence Day story, the author explained, and I had only a very short time in which to sell it.

The author was mistaken. I had quite a long time to sell the story—more than seven months. This December, we'll resurrect the story from our files, where it has lain ever since we broke the sad news to the writer, and offer it for sale.

Holiday yarns are all right to write, provided you do them only rarely, because, of course, only one holiday story is used in the issue which comes out around that holiday. You must, however, get them out to market well in advance.

Most monthly magazines work around four months in advance; the weeklies work around three months in advance. They're particularly careful, in addition, about holiday stories: if they make it a practice to run a Christmas story in their December issues, as most magazines do, they'll start shopping for one around July or August. There's a joke in the trade about a writer describing snow slopes and the sting of sleet in a story while sitting in his undershorts and cursing the 102-degree temperature.

Start your holiday stories moving around the magazines five or six months before the holiday is due to turn up. No editor will think you silly if your Easter story shows up in September; he'll think you silly only if it arrives in March or April. The same rule applies if you do seasonal stories of any kind. Get busy on your football stories while the baseball season is in full swing and begin work on your baseball stories the day Yale pits its eleven against Harvard.

There are exceptions, of course. Last year, one major magazine looked around for quite a while without locating a suitable Christmas story and then phoned agents frantically late in November asking if they could scare up a yarn at once. Sometimes an editor will see a piece out of season or otherwise unusable in the near future and like it so much he'll buy it and hold it a year or more before using it. (Once one magazine was overloaded with yarns concerned with a specific aspect of witchcraft but liked one we showed them so much that they bought it and held it for four years before they were able to publish it. These, however, are the exceptions which prove the rule.)

And that, by the way, is the theme of this chapter, and of much of this book. The best bets—the proven methods—are the ones to be followed. You may, if you like, be contrary and follow the exceptions, but you'll find, all too soon, that the weeks in which you earn enough to eat will be exceptions too.

4

THE INSIDE STORY: *Behind editorial doors*

At least one story in every hundred offered to editors contains a page which is upside down or two pages which are stuck together at one corner with a light dab of glue. This is an ancient wheeze coined around 1850, although many new writers using it believe they've just invented the idea, and it is designed to determine whether or not the editor has read the script. The theory, of course, is that the editor has not read the script if it is returned, rejected, with the page still reversed or the two pages still stuck together.

Aside from the fact that that isn't necessarily so, because experienced editors can sometimes tell that a script isn't for them after they've seen the first two pages or even the first two paragraphs, there's no real point in it. You may take my word for it that, with exceptions so very rare that they're not worth worrying about, every script submitted to a publishing house is read—or, at least, enough of it is read to determine whether or not it should be bought or returned.

It is frustrating to realize that the script over which you've labored so hard may not be read beyond the first page when you offer it for sale, and it is frustrating to get it back with a printed rejection slip which gives you no clue to the reasons for rejection, but it results from the fact that the editor is an extremely busy man whose only reason for looking at the script at all is the hope that he can buy it. If a quick look or a full reading assures him that he cannot, he tosses it aside and hurries on to the next script. He can afford to take time to write a note only when he believes a script can be fixed up and made purchasable or when a script isn't right that time but the author is sufficiently close that he may make the grade next time.

Over lunch the other day, a well-known editor explained his problems thoroughly while reminiscing about his start at his job.

"The first day I turned up at the office," he said, "I was determined to read every script from first page to last, and write a letter of analysis with every script I turned down. I'd done some free-lance writing and I knew how a printed rejection slip could sock you in the stomach. There were about a hundred scripts waiting to be read." He sighed. "By noon, I'd read six of them thoroughly, even though I could tell almost from the start of each one that they weren't for us, and I'd written long letters of criticism—and then Joey, our office boy, walked in. He had another sixty scripts and a note from the publisher discussing my current duties. I had an appointment with the art director to discuss some illustrations, an appointment with one of the boys in the advertising department to discuss some ad space he wanted, an appointment with a well-known writer who was in town, an appointment with an agent who'd begun a fight for a rate raise for a client with the former editor and wanted to finish it with me, and four other appointments—all for that afternoon. Not to mention a couple of little jobs like make-up and writing captions.

"Well," said the editor, "for a couple of minutes I sat there and wanted to cut my throat. Then I grabbed a big pile of manuscripts and began to read like hell. The minute I saw for sure that a script was a turndown, I stuck a rejection slip on it."

Let's suppose, as happens far more frequently than you might think, an editor who puts out a magazine composed entirely of science-fiction stories looks over a submission and sees that it is a love story or a detective story. There's no reason in the world to read that script thoroughly; his job is to find enough stories of the right type to get out his magazine and still manage to do the hundred jobs other than reading which are a part of the task of getting his magazine out. Let's suppose that he sees after a few pages that a script is too clumsily written or plotted for purchase, or that it is based on a subject which is taboo in his market (there's a chapter about specific editorial taboos later on, by the way), or that, in short, the script—for any reason whatever—is one he cannot buy or have the author fix. He won't read *those* scripts all the way through; his time limits and the press of other business won't let him. He will, however, read a close-but-not-quite script all the way through, perhaps even twice, before turning it down, and he'll always try to write a little note of encouragement or scribble a few words on the rejection slip, to an author who is close—for the simple business reason that he must have good stories to fill his magazine. Sometimes he's so rushed with other work that there's no time even for little notes of encouragement; he just sends the script back and hopes the author will keep plugging until he makes the grade.

Because of time tightness, most publishing houses work on a two-pile basis: the rush pile and unrush or slush pile system. Under this method, all scripts which arrive are sorted before reading into two groups. Into the rush pile go stories by authors who have sold to the magazine in the past, stories by authors who have not sold to the magazine before but are well-known, and stories submitted by good agents. Stories by new writers who are recommended by established authors also usually go into the rush pile. The unrush or slush pile draws stories by unfamiliar names and stories submitted by new agents who are unknown to the editor.

The rush pile, for cold-blooded business reasons, gets the first and fastest reading, because the editor knows he will get a good percentage of acceptable stories from it. Authors who have sold to his market or to similar markets in the past and agents from whom he buys regularly can usually be expected to turn up with good stuff. Rush pile buying is heavy.

Subsequently the editor turns to the unrush pile and here the buying is lighter. Many stories, as described, get the quick brushoff: they obviously aren't right. Others are read and put aside for a later rereading; they aren't quite right but perhaps the author can fix them up or perhaps they should be rejected and the author encouraged to try again. And others are read and placed at once in the acceptance basket, while the editor makes a mental note that that boy goes into the rush pile in the future.

There used to be a legend that some editors would reject three or four perfectly acceptable stories by a new writer before buying one in order to determine whether or not the author was consistent and could be depended upon to keep turning out good stories. Don't you believe it. Editors desire consistency in an author because the man who can help fill their magazines issue after issue is valuable, but they're not going to pass up good stories and, perhaps, watch a rival magazine snap them up and get first look at the author's stuff in the future.

Besides, purchase of stories by new writers is important for three good reasons. For one thing, new writers' stories may be purchased at bottom rates, which helps balance the budget and fit in higher-priced stories by name writers. For another, new writers are needed to replace established authors who have died, or retired, or moved to other fields, and, also, they frequently turn out to be as good as, or better than, the established authors in the field. And, finally, editors who regularly discover new writers who become established names bolster their own reputations, and make their own jobs additionally secure. You may be sure that an editor is always happy to buy a story by a new writer and will promptly grasp the opportunity to do so.

At the smaller houses, a single editor reads both the rush and unrush piles and handles every other job involved in getting out the magazine as well. At some of the pulp houses, some editors are charged with the job of getting out an entire group of magazines single-handed. At some of the larger houses, a group reads the unrush, and the managing editor, or editor-in-chief, reads the rush and those scripts selected from the other pile by his staff; at others, one group of editors divides up the rush (each editor usually handling stories from specific agents and authors, plus a percentage of the unexpected rush) and another group reads the unknown writers' material, and the chief editor reads and approves or disapproves for purchase the selected stories from either group. A few magazines have editorial boards which approve or disapprove stories selected for purchase by preliminary staff readers.

These mass-reading setups frequently worry writers who fear that their stories' sales chances are reduced by the necessity of being passed by a number of different people. Actually this fear is almost groundless. Editors on the same magazine hunt for the same kinds of stories on the same quality levels and a story which one experienced editor likes will usually be liked equally by all the other men and women on the staff.

When a story is accepted, a voucher is filled out and sent through to the accounting department, the bookkeeper, the publisher, or whoever is charged with disbursing funds for the firm. At one time, most firms made payment promptly after publication of the story, and in some cases not so very promptly. Today, with very few exceptions, most firms pay on acceptance —which actually means after the voucher has made its required rounds and been acted upon, a matter of anywhere from one day to about three weeks. Where the firm has an involved disbursement system, or where the disbursement system *could* be rapid but the man who pays always has to wrestle with himself for a while before he shells out, the editor will usually drop you a note to tell you that the story had been accepted and the check will be along after a while.

The story itself is placed in the editorial safe—a real safe in some cases, a desk drawer in others—and held there until the balance of the magazine permits the editor to schedule it. Then the script is sent or given to an artist, who draws an illustration for it (some magazines, incidentally, get the illustration before they schedule a yarn); the script is returned to the editor or a member of his staff, who writes the blurbs for it—the little descriptive paragraphs which appear in the magazine on the opening page of the story, and sometimes on the contents page; the story is sent with the others to the printers; galleys come back from the printers and are proofread and okayed; and finally the magazine comes out and shows up at your local newsstand, where you have been camping for the past two months waiting for it.

It never does any harm to drop the editor a little note—which does not mean an eight-page affair detailing your struggles in the writing business—thanking him for the check. Comparatively few writers do this, but I've watched editors' faces light up when a nice note does arrive.

That's the letter to send after your story is bought; the kind of letter to send when you're offering a story is another question again. Fully 90 per cent of the letters accompanying new writers' submissions state nothing more, when boiled down, than the fact that the writer is submitting herewith a story. This sort of letter should not be sent at all. If the editor's eyeglasses are good enough to enable him to see at all, they are good enough to show him that you have sent a story and not an elephant or a sport shirt. The rule is simple enough: if you have nothing to say, don't say it.

Anything which will get you on the rush pile or anything which may in any way favorably increase your chances of sale is certainly adequate reason for enclosing a letter. The former is quite possible, so by all means remind the editor casually that he previously bought a story from you, or that you have sold twenty stories to other magazines in the same field, or that W. Somerset Maugham suggested you send the story along and a separate introductory letter from Maugham will be arriving shortly. The latter is practically impossible; don't try it unless you are able to remind the editor that you are his wife's adored kid brother, or that you happen to have a picture of him with a blonde at "21" when his wife thought he was working late, or that your father happens to be president of the bank at which he has just requested a personal loan. These are the only three cases which can favorably increase the chances of a story's sale; otherwise, unless you have some specific background, as described, which will get you on the rush pile, don't write a letter at all.

And don't, whatever you do, enclose a letter instructing the editor to purchase the story because you have seen far worse in his magazine. This will bring your story home promptly, possibly accompanied by a lit stick of dynamite.

Aside from the obvious diplomatic error in informing an editor that he occasionally publishes rotten stories, or that he usually publishes rotten stories, the chances are more than excellent that you may be wrong. You may, for one thing, not be experienced enough to judge whether or not a story is good, especially in the sense of whether or not a particular audience will like it. You may, for another, never become experienced enough, for it is a truism of this business that many first-grade writers are never able to evaluate correctly another writer's work or, for that matter, their own.

When one very well-known client brings in a new story and raves about it, I can usually be sure it will be a dud; when he brings in a new story with a glum or apologetic look on his face, it usually sells promptly and receives public acclaim. I know a hundred other writers with the same knack for prophecy in reverse.

You may, of course, be absolutely right in your analysis. Few editors consistently buy bad stories they believe are good and continue to hold their jobs; but sometimes circumstances force editors to buy and publish some stories they *know* are third-rate.

Sometimes, for example, an editor will get a run of just-fair stories for a long period, and pass them all up in the hope that better stuff will come in. Then, suddenly, he'll find himself up against a deadline, with not enough purchased material on hand to fill an issue—and he'll have to run around frantically and buy several of the least awful stories in the right lengths or types which are then on his submission piles. The stories he buys may be even worse than those he had by-passed a few weeks before, but he's in a jam and he has no choice.

Sometimes an editor will give an assignment to an old reliable author who has written for his magazine for years, and Old Reliable, who has never let him down before, suddenly gets sick and fails to produce. The editor has no choice other than to fill the hole with the best possible yarn of the same length or type he can find in a hurry and that best possible yarn may not be so good. Sometimes a publishing house executive will horn into editorial department matters and insist that an inferior story by a friend be published; one such executive with stock in the company was recently kicked upstairs, away from editorial matters entirely, because he had done this several times.

These are, of course, just the other side of the coin to the reasons for the occasional rejection of good stories for reasons other than quality: taboo, overstock, etc. Circumstances under which bad stories are bought are rare and may occur only a few times in a lifetime; it would be silly to depend on them. Better try to get your stories into the circumstances under which *most* stories are bought: because they're first-grade stories.

When you submit a story to a magazine, by the way, you should have a report on it in two to four weeks, exclusive of mail travel time. Don't, however, automatically assume that a story is sold if a number of months pass without a report; silence for this length of time is extremely rare, but it may mean nothing more than the fact that there have been several illnesses or vacations in the editorial department.

Your best bet, any way you look at it, is to force yourself to forget a script the moment it is put into the mail and concentrate on writing new material. You'll know what has happened to it when you find an editorial check in your mailbox.

5

INSPIRATION, PERSPIRATION, DESPERATION:
Working habits

The writing life looks easy to the nonwriter. All you have to do, he says, eyeing you enviously, is sit down at a typewriter every once in a while and pound out a little story and go and collect a big check for it. No time clocks; no bosses; no one to tell you what to do and when to do it.

The working writer, however, knows that the job of pounding out that little story is anything but easy, particularly after he has passed the beginner's stage where any careless mass of wordage he has produced looks like a good story to him, and he has begun to work in the professional, planned way which produces salable material. He also knows that the complete lack of time clocks and bosses in the writing business, in addition to being its most wonderful aspect, can frequently be its biggest headache.

When a bookkeeper comes to the office and doesn't feel much like keeping the books that day, he keeps them anyway because he knows the boss will bawl him out or fire him if he is caught sitting around drawing doodles. As a result, the work gets done. The full- or part-time writer, however, is his own boss in his writing work, and too often the work does not get done.

Through the years, writers have invented a multitude of excuses and delaying actions to avoid settling down to the man-sized job of turning out that salable story, with their chief ally the conclusion that writing is a delicate mental undertaking which can easily go awry if conditions are not exactly right. Among the devices employed are the wait for inspiration, the presence of that awry picture on the wall which will jar if it isn't straightened, the necessity for sharpening those jarringly blunt pencils (even though you type your stuff and practically never use the pencils), the lack of a really suitable hideaway in which to write, the fact that you were out late the previous night and your mind isn't as clear and sharp as necessary, the fact that you had a hard day at the office and your stuff won't be done real justice if you undertake your spare-time writing stint that evening, the noise your family or the neighbor's children are making, and the fact that the stuff just doesn't seem to be coming right that day so what's the sense in continuing? There are about a hundred others; if you have a writer's active imagination, you'll think them up yourself.

Well, your friends and family aren't listening right now, so let me state it bluntly: most of these are just as make-believe as those fiction stories you write.

If you will force yourself to work out those story ideas without waiting for inspiration to slosh you across the back of the head, and if you will force yourself to write one sentence after another despite the fact that the picture is awry and the pencils are blunt, and your family is making an awful racket, and you're writing in one corner of a bedroom instead of a big soundproof study, and you had a big night with the boys last night, and the stuff looks awful as you write it, you will find— when you examine it a day or two later—that the material you've produced is exactly as good or bad as the material you normally produce, or would produce under the most ideal conditions.

Naturally, you will do good work on some days and not-so-good work on others; science is constantly seeking to discover— though it has not yet succeeded—why people in every trade and profession do excellent work at certain times and not-so-excellent work at others. The important thing is that the excuses upon which writers so often seize to avoid doing work usually have very little to do with it. If you keep a careful check list, you will find, as years pass, that some of your best work was produced under working conditions which were very poor, and that some of your worst stories were written while you were working under conditions which were absolutely ideal.

The best cure for the habit of literary procrastination, and the best way to avoid the habit if you have not yet fallen into it, is the stern and rigid working schedule: the setting of specific hours during which you must sit and write. If you do this, and abide rigidly by the schedule, you will get your work done because you are forcing yourself to be as tough a boss to yourself as a boss in a standard business is to his employees.

Many new writers are shocked at the notion of a writing schedule, and feel they simply can't write that way. This is usually just another subconscious excuse, because working under a rigid schedule means working, and can usually be dismissed by a little honest self-questioning and a little logic. After all, when you get right down to it, why can't you? When you attend school, you're under a rigid schedule: you begin work at a specific hour and stop work at a specific hour and work steadily during those hours. When you have a job, you begin and end at set times and work with reasonable steadiness in between. And if you're married and your job is homemaking, you still work on a fairly rigid schedule: preparing the meals and cleaning and doing the other household chores at specific times.

It adds up exactly the same way, except that in school and as an employee, you have teachers and truant officers and bosses to watch over you, and, as a housewife, there are the children and your husband to complain if the meals aren't ready on time or if the clothes aren't kept mended and clean. You're on your own as a writer, and you'll get your work done if you set up that harsh boss, the religiously followed schedule, to keep you working hard.

When you set up a schedule, don't go overboard with it. It is designed to keep you working hard, but not so abnormally hard that you can't possibly keep up with it for long. Set it so that you get in as much work as you can handle, not any more and not any less. If you're a part-time writer, two or three hours an evening for about three evenings a week is plenty; more than that will make your combined jobs so great a strain on your physical and mental health that you soon won't be able to do either. If you're a full-time writer, from nine or ten to five, five days a week, with an hour off for lunch, is adequate.

All things considered, there is only one kind of writer who should not use the schedule system: the writer who discovers, after extended tryouts of both systems, that he really gets more work done by going to the typewriter at unspecified periods, and who is a good enough self-disciplinarian to spend plenty of total time at his typewriter. If you find that you are really in this small group—and make sure you aren't just talking yourself into it to get away from a tough boss—go ahead and work that way.

Otherwise, stick to a schedule, and force yourself to write steadily during the hours you have set for yourself. You'll find that regular writing will turn into a habit, and that's a wonderful thing.

The motion pictures frequently depict writers as hard-drinking men, and sometimes as comic drunks. There's nothing comic about it. Too many top-grade writers have risen high in their professions and then sunk back into failure because of their overfondness for patronizing the package stores.

I said a little while ago that you needn't fear to work the morning after a big evening with the boys, and that still goes. If you're reasonably normal, your mind isn't so weak that a frolicsome night will make it function so fuzzily that it will impair the quality of your stuff. The mental fuzziness which comes from habitual drinking, however, is another story entirely.

When you begin to hit the bottle too regularly, you can kiss your writing career good-by and reserve a hallway in Skid Row for sleeping purposes. I don't know why many new writers believe they must drink heavily as part of their chosen profession; perhaps it is because writing is a romantic trade, and some of them think there is also something disreputably romantic and freethinking about being the bad boy or girl who drinks. Perish that thought: your colleagues in the adjoining beds of the drunk wards will number some of the weakest minded and least romantic individuals in your city.

Most important, don't ever drink at all—not even an eye-dropper's worth—when you are working, particularly if you ever get the bright idea of doing so to speed up your thinking or writing. You'll speed up at first, all right, but after a while you'll find yourself having to drink more and more to be able to write less and less. Soon you won't be able to write at all without drinking; and a little later you won't be able to write at all.

The same applies to Benzedrine, stay-awake pills, and all other artificial stimulants. You're better off staying away from them entirely, and certainly while you are writing. Most writers have made their way through the stimulus of their natural abilities, and so can you.

Sometimes, when you have left an incomplete story alone for a while, you will return to it to find that it has cooled off. You just can't seem to get started again; you just can't seem to return to the mood.

There are several professional tricks designed to prevent an occurrence of this sort, and to combat it if it does happen. The best of these is one which works to keep it from happening at all.

When you're hot in the middle of a story, and you note the arrival of your schedule end or the time you have been planning to quit, the natural tendency is to keep working as long as things are going so well. It's natural, but it may be a mistake. Stop right there—right in the middle of a sentence, or even in the middle of a word.

When you keep going until you finish the scene or sequence on which you're working, the job before you next time is almost equivalent to that of starting an entirely new story. You've got to make a fresh beginning, pretty much, with a new scene, and it isn't surprising if you find it hard to do when you next come to your typewriter. When you stop in midsentence or midword, however, your mind has already preceded you—and you know just what you have to write. You sit down at the typewriter and finish the word, sentence, and paragraph, and you can usually swing on from there into the rest of the story.

If you stopped at the end of a scene last time, and just can't get going this time, take the last page you'd written, lay it alongside your typewriter, and begin to retype it. By the time you've completed the retyping, you'll be in the swing of the yarn again, and can go on from there.

And if that doesn't work, you'll have to do something drastic. It will tear your heart apart to do it, but do it if it is absolutely necessary. Take the last page of that story, rip it into small pieces, and throw it away. Don't throw it in your wastebasket; throw it out your window or flush it down the drain—anywhere where you will no longer have the temptation to snatch it up again and glue it together.

Then begin to write that page all over again. Don't try to write it word for word the same as the last time; write it as though you're doing something entirely new. You'd already thought this page out when you wrote it the last time, however, and, as you work now, its phrasing and handling will come easily. You'll usually be able to finish it and keep going without pausing at the point where you stopped last time.

Big brother to the miniature work stoppage is the slump, the complete inability to work which is supposed to strike most writers at least once in a lifetime, and which may last for months. Slumps are a favorite topic of conversation among writers, and I know a great many who have had them and suffered greatly while in the throes. You, however, can avoid them entirely by considering them squarely and recognizing them for what they are: the familiar subconscious why-I-should-stay-away-from-the-typewriter impulse, as described earlier in this chapter, enormously magnified by the writer's imagination.

A slump may be compared, in a way, to the paralyzed arm of a mental patient, who has convinced himself so thoroughly that his arm is paralyzed that he will not feel a lighted match pressed against it. You get dramatic proof of the lack of real paralysis, however, as I once did in the company of a client who writes medical material, when you watch the patient gravely wave his paralyzed arm up and down to show you how freely it used to move before the paralysis set in. There's an old joke to this effect, probably based on this sort of actual occurrence, which has been observed many times by psychiatrists.

The slump is every bit as real to the writer, who suffers agonies trying to snap out of it. He tries over and over again to write, but he's licked before he starts; he just knows he's in a slump and can't write, so of course he can't. Eventually, his mind will succeed in casting off the idiot notion that his writing ability has miraculously vanished without rhyme or reason, and he is all right again: but there's no necessity to wait that long, or to allow the slump to start at all.

At least ten times, clients have come to my office and told me they're in a serious slump, and asked if I will advance them some money to pay their bills until they snap out of it. My answer is usually the same: I tell them they've talked themselves into their slumps, and that they can have the money if they will go into a vacant office in my suite and write a story whose sale will cover the amount advanced to them. Then I accompany them while they go into the office, and watch them pace back and forth for a while, and sit down in the chair and leap up again a few times, and finally begin painfully to write, cursing and groaning that the stuff is terrible and incoherent, as it has been every time they've tried, lately. Of course it isn't— it's a little rusty, perhaps, but generally in line with the quality of their output during normal periods. I prod them some more, and they keep working; and after a whole they're typing away rapidly, and the slump's back is cracked. I usually give them one final bawling-out before they leave with my check to pay their past-due bills, to make sure they don't go home afterward and start the whole thing all over again.

Remember one thing if you feel a slump coming on: writing ability isn't a shallow pan of water. It doesn't evaporate suddenly, and it doesn't dry up or get used out. (Investigate the few cases of writers who've "written themselves out" and vanished from the magazine pages, and you'll find that each one vanished because he refused or unwittingly failed to adjust himself to new trends, or because he simply talked himself into believing that he was written out—a condition related to the slump—and will be back once the illusion fades.) If you force yourself to write and, most important, to complete stories, however awful they may seem to you at the time, your slump will go just as it came.

One more psychological hurdle you'll want to jump is first-draftitis, the habit of writing loosely and carelessly because you know you can fix everything up in subsequent drafts. This one is a progressive disease: you'll find yourself writing more and more loosely and carelessly all the time, until your first drafts resemble nothing normal and require two dozen additional drafts to be made to look like stories.

It's dangerous stuff. You get into the habit of using unsatisfactory words or phrases or sentences or paragraphs because you feel that you can fix them up when you go over the yarn, and, before you know it, you can't come up with suitable words or phrases or sentences or paragraphs when you want them. What you have done is blunt your naturally sharp word sense and feeling for language by too lax acceptance of substitutes when you should have been insisting on the originals.

The way to safeguard against this error is to write each page of your first draft as tightly and carefully as if it had to be sent to the editor the moment it was pulled out of the type-writer. It may slow you up a bit at first, but the net result— the habit of careful, tight writing—will be well worth it.

A great many writers insure this by actually making the first draft their final draft: by typing right on white paper, accom-panied by carbon and second sheet for the author's file copy, and sending their material to editors exactly as written. You may be unwilling to go to this extreme, and there's really no harm in allowing yourself a second draft in which you retype and make minor corrections.

But stop dead and get it straight the first time if you ever catch yourself thinking that something isn't right but you can always fix it in the next draft.

6

YOUR ATTRACTIVE MERCHANDISE:
The professional-looking manuscript

The average editor's second home is his oculist's office. He goes there all too often for the treatment of eyestrain and related ailments, the result of the fact that every facet of his work—manuscript reading, proofreading of galleys, okaying of artwork, reading of correspondence, blurb writing, etc.—requires constant and steady use of his eyes. Not all editorial offices are the way they look in the movies, either, and sometimes the lighting in his sanctum sanctorum is very poor.

You can understand, therefore, why he will be unhappy if you send him a sloppy manuscript which is hard to read and which makes his aching eyes ache all the more. He may be the fairest minded man in the world, but he will still find himself putting your script back at the bottom of the reading pile the first three or four times he comes to it, and then, when he does finally read it, he'll give it a far more cursory, fate-already-sealed examination than the other manuscripts in the pile. Several editors have stated publicly that the content is the thing, and that they would buy a good story if it came in written with a thick crayon on wrapping paper; but try and get them to name just one sloppy manuscript they've actually bought in the past decade.

Most professionals realize this. They know that, though of course the writing and handling are the important things, there is a sort of psychological advantage in a beautifully prepared manuscript, and that a good story in sloppy manuscript form somehow seems less good—and they go out of their way to make sure that their scripts are as first-grade in appearance as in content. Stop tapping your foot impatiently, therefore, and thinking that manuscript preparation is minor stuff: nothing which may mean the difference between a prejudiced or unprejudiced reading is minor.

On pages 61 to 63, I have included samples of the way the first and subsequent pages of your manuscripts should look. Use them as a guide, and keep the following important facts in mind:

1. Don't send handwritten manuscripts to editors. Type your manuscripts, or get someone to retype for you if you handwrite your stuff. Some editors won't read handwritten material at all; none will read handwritten material as happily as typewritten material. Some small magazines, as a matter of fact, can't buy handwritten stories even if they want to do so: they have no facilities for retyping the stuff or getting it retyped, and they cannot send handwritten stories to their printers. (Many printers' contracts contain a clause stating that they will not set from handwritten copy.)

2. Use a good grade of bond paper containing at least 25 per cent rag or cotton, rather than sulphite paper, so that you can make erasures without blurring your words or rubbing holes in your manuscripts. The difference in price between rag and sulphite papers is moderate, and worth it. Don't, however, swing too far in the other direction and use one of those ultra-crinkly kinds of paper which cost about a nickel a sheet and look as though the government uses them to make currency. Pros who write regularly can't afford this kind of stuff, and it will mark you as a beginner.

3. Use standard 8½ x 11 paper, and not legal or some other unusual size which won't fit in the editor's in-basket, desk drawer, or brief case. Sixteen-pound is best; twenty-pound costs

too much in the mails, and a lighter weight paper creases and tears too easily.

4. Get the gum and the goo out of your keys before you type the copy you're going to send to the editor. A good stiff typewriter brush and some carbon tet will do it, and the editor won't have to tear his hair out trying to decide whether those shapeless little blobs are *a*'s, *e*'s, *o*'s, *s*'s, or *c*'s, and whether or not he ought to go up to your place and stuff your manuscript down your throat.

5. Double-space your sheet, and leave at least one inch of white space on all sides, as shown. If the editor buys your manuscript, he'll need room to make corrections and alterations, if any, and write his instructions to the printer.

6. When you come to an inch or so from the bottom of the page, just stop and go on to the next page; don't write "more." That's all right in newspaper writing, where each paragraph of a story contains less important facts than the previous one, and your story can end practically anywhere; but there's something wrong with your magazine yarn if the editor can't tell there's more when he comes to the bottom of a page.

7. When you come to the end of your story, just stop, or go down five single spaces and type a few dashes or "The End." Don't write 30, which means the end only to people familiar with newspaper tradition, and don't, if you want the editor to take you seriously, write "Finis."

8. As shown, put your real name and address in the upper left-hand corner of the first page, so that the editor will know where and to whom to send the check if the story is bought; if you're using a pseudonym, put it under the title—otherwise put you real name there too. If you work through an agent, put your name in the upper left-hand corner, but leave out your address —make it in care of your agent's name and address. That will give the editor the go-ahead to negotiate with your agent if he wants to buy your yarn.

9. Put only the approximate word count in the upper right-

hand corner: leave off such beginner's favorites as "For Sale" or "Usual Rates." The editor is aware that your script is for sale and not for rent or just to be admired, and he has his business office to remind him not to pay unusual rates. If you have a special reason for wishing to reserve certain rights—for example, if you're a movie or television writer who does an occasional magazine piece, and you also want to adapt the yarn for your own regular medium—mention this in an accompanying note or underneath the word count; otherwise, leave it out entirely. Don't list an arbitrary restriction, such as, "First Upper Half of Eastern New York State Rights Only," without reason; nearly all magazines have regular specific rights which they always buy, and they'd just as soon by-pass your story as argue with you. Most of them, however, will return unused rights upon request after they publish your yarn.

If you have an agent, of course, let him worry about the rights. That's part of his job.

10. The word count, incidentally, should be to the nearest hundred or fifty; it need not be something like "4,673," which necessitates counting every word. You get the word count by counting several typical pages, arriving at a typical amount of words per page, and multiplying it by the amount of pages in the story. You'll have to count the first and last pages, since they'll probably be shorter; and take off about fifty words for each page with an excessive amount of dialogue. Another good way to count your wordage rapidly is to count the amount of words in several typical lines, arrive at a typical amount per line, and multiply it by the amount of lines in the story. Many writers speed up this latter system by setting their typewriters and marking the paper so that they get an equal number of lines on all but the first and last pages.

11. A cover page at the back and front of the manuscript isn't a bad idea, since it will keep the script clean through a good many submissions. Don't decorate it in any way, however; your name and address and the title of the story is sufficient.

If you work through an agent, skip the cover pages; he puts your script in a heavy cardboard or leatherette folder which protects it.

12. Don't secure copyright and list this on your script. There is practically no piracy whatever in the publishing business these days, and besides, under law, the very fact of your authorship gives you an automatic or common-law copyright. The purchasing magazine will copyright the story along with the rest of the issue's contents when they publish it, and to secure copyright beforehand and list it is the sure sign of the amateur.

13. Fasten your story with a loose paper clip only; never with a paper fastener or any other device which punches through the pages. Editors like to remove the clip when they read a yarn, so they can flick the pages around freely. Paper fasteners and staples are hard to get out and sometimes cut the fingers, evoking much lack of merriment.

14. Get the name of your story and the page number, as shown, on the second page and every page thereafter. Sometimes the editor will pick up a batch of stories and drop them all, scattering the pages all over the floor. He'll be grateful if the pages are identified and he can piece the stories together rapidly.

15. Either the pica or the elite type face is acceptable to editors, provided it is clean and provided it is orthodox. Don't use special or fancy typewriters such as those which type all in italics, or all in capitals, or in Old English; they distract the editor while he's trying to read your story, which is the one thing you don't want to do. For the same reason, the ribbon should be medium-inked and black, not heavily and smudgily inked and blue or green or purple or brown with yellow polka dots.

16. In general, keep in mind the fact that the primary function and purpose of the physical arrangement and appearance of your manuscript is to permit the editor to read it as easily and with as little distraction as possible. Such things as artistic

borders drawn around the text will distract the editor; therefore, they're not to be used. Guide yourself with the rule that the neatest and most businesslike manuscript is the best-looking manuscript.

17. Type only on one side of the paper.

18. Don't quote a price for your manuscript, either on the script or in an accompanying letter. Most magazines have set rates of payment; if not, the editor will prefer to make an offer.

19. If you want to emphasize a word or sentence or bit of dialogue, underline it, and it will be set up in italics when published. (*This sentence is in italics.*) If you leave out a word while typing, strike a diagonal (/) in the space in which it belongs and type the word in the line above. A listing of proofreaders' marks can be found in any good dictionary, but use these only in the cases where the galleys of your material are sent to you for correction. (This is usually done with books, only very rarely done with magazine material.) If there are a number of errors on pages of your manuscript, don't use proofreaders' marks; retype the pages.

20. When you are quoting something like a letter or a newspaper clipping in a manuscript, don't distinguish it from the rest of the script by typing it in single space. Nothing at all in your manuscript should ever be typed in single space. Just indent an additional five spaces to the right of your regular paragraph indentation, and start your letter there. The different margin arrangement will make it stand out.

21. Indent your paragraphs from five to seven spaces. Leave one space between words (not two, as a great many new writers do, for no discernible reason) and two spaces between sentences.

22. Generally, more writers use portables than standard models of typewriters, probably because they can be carted along when the owners wish to get a little writing done on trips and vacations. Almost every firm, incidentally, puts out a writers' model which includes such things as ready-made ex-

clamation points (so that you don't have to bother stopping and holding one finger on your space bar while you hit the apostrophe and period with another), accent marks, etc. These cost a little more than the regular models.

23. A number of people in the field believe that a heavy manuscript must be mailed flat, but that a manuscript of less than a dozen pages may be folded in half or in thirds. Judging from the reactions of most editors, who hate folded scripts because they're harder to handle and because they start to curl, my own impression is that scripts should always be mailed flat. The only difference in cost is the slightly higher prices of large envelopes which will hold unfolded scripts, and this is so negligible that you'd be wise to play it safe and always mail your scripts flat. Don't forget to enclose a stamped, self-addressed return envelope with each submission—and make sure it is large enough to hold the script.

24. Keep a carbon copy of every script you send to market. Scripts get lost, shortened through the loss of pages in the editorial offices, and, if the editor reads at home and has a dog or an ungovernable temper, chewed up. It's an unhappy thing to lose a good story for which you have no copy, or to sell a copyless story to an editor and have him lose page 14 and wire you to rush your carbon of the page at once.

25. And, finally, make sure that you have a fresh, not-too-far-gone ribbon in your typewriter when you're preparing your final copy, so that your machine will do more than make faint indentations in the paper. Remember the editor's sore eyes?

Jonathan C. Rogers
5575 North Conroy Drive
Hartsdale, New York

approx. 4,700 words

A SECRET FOR RITA

by Ken Morrow

Norcross stood there in the darkness for a moment, afraid to move and too nervous to stand still. Then, as the sounds in the hallway increased, he got down on his knees in the darkness and began to crawl forward, slowly, soundlessly.

He was halfway across the corridor when lights suddenly flared, and a beefy hand gripped the back of his neck. He knew from the enormous strength of the hand that it could belong to no one but Joseph J. O'Hara.

O'Hara's voice confirmed it. "Norcross! It isn't possible!"

Norcross got to his feet, and squirmed out of O'Hara's grasp to face him. He grinned feebly.

"Yes, it is, Mr. O'Hara," he said. "I was just going, though."

A SECRET FOR RITA -- 2

O'Hara gripped his shirtfront. "Wasn't last
night enough for you?" he roared.

"Plenty, Mr. O'Hara," Norcross said. He tried
to detach the fingers. "I was just going, anyway."

"You're not going anywhere yet," O'Hara said.
He thrust his red face closer. "What are you
doing in my apartment tonight, you miserable little
flat-faced moron?"

"I was just going, Mr. O'Hara...."

"I asked you a question!" O'Hara roared.

Norcross winced, and made a final effort to
release himself from the other man's grasp. Not
a chance.

"Well, I'll tell you, Mr. O'Hara," he said,
finally. "I came here to see if I could talk to
Rita."

There was a long, dead silence, punctuated
only by the sound of O'Hara's rasping breath.
Then O'Hara broke it, his voice curiously soft and
gentle.

"Did Rita let you in, Norcross?" he asked.

"No, sir," Norcross said. "She doesn't seem
to be here."

A SECRET FOR RITA -- 3

"Did my wife let you in, Norcross?" he asked.

"No, sir. She doesn't seem to be here, either."

"Then may I ask," O'Hara said gently, "how you got into my apartment?"

Norcross wiped a bead of sweat off his upper lip. "I climbed in through your living-room window," he said. "It was open."

O'Hara's mouth was open, too. It hung that way for a while as he stared at Norcross.

"You should be careful about those things, Mr. O'Hara," Norcross went on, eagerly. "There are burglars in this town. Leaving windows open is a dangerous thing to..."

"Shuddup!" O'Hara howled. Then his voice quieted again. "Did you know you can get ten years for entering my apartment through a window that way, Norcross?" he asked. "Did you know I can call a cop and have you put away for ten long years?"

"Mr. O'Hara! You wouldn't!"

A dangerous grin lit up O'Hara's face. "No," he said. "I'm going to take you by the scruff of

7

SHORT CUTS TO THE SCRAP HEAP:
Taboos

Tell me, how do you feel about polygamy? Does the idea of one man with a variety of wives, or one woman with a small army of husbands, offend your moral sense?

Most people feel that it does, and, as a result, polygamy is a taboo subject. You will rarely see a multiple marriage story in print.

Taboo restrictions, for the most part, are the KEEP OUT signs to subjects which, editors and publishers have found through the years, offend the moral sensitivities of the public (or of the public's moral guardians, such as churches, decency groups, and censors), or which in any other way mar the public's enjoyment of the material offered. Let's have a look at them.

Pansies of the nonfloral variety are taboo for obvious moral reasons, even when treated humorously, as are all other types of sexual abnormality, such as incest, sodomy, or rape. I refer here, as I've said, primarily to the slicks and pulps; the quality magazines still face the seamiest sides of life far more squarely. Common-law marriage, the keeping of mistresses, and prostitution have begun to receive increased attention in the slick magazines, but they are usually still taboo when treated too casually or approvingly. The practice, generally, is to present these things as existing aspects of life, but to show them as disruptive rather than desirable. Excessive drinking scenes aren't wanted, especially when the author treats excessive drinking sympathetically or as the thing to do, and neither are scenes of extreme brutality or sadism. Miscegenation and artificial insemination are taboo.

Stories which laugh or sneer at cripples, or at people with deformities or facial blemishes, or at people with afflictions such as stuttering are in bad taste and therefore taboo. Stories which advocate religious bias or racial prejudice, or which encourage atheism, won't go. Other morally taboo subjects are those which encourage lawlessness or any other kinds of morally offensive acts; such as pro-lynching stories, stories which advocate mercy killings, or stories which show criminals in a favorable and sympathetic light.

Subjects which are taboo because they mar enjoyment, but don't necessarily offend the moral sense, would include, for example, those which deal with snakes or rats. Most people feel crawly when they read about these creatures, and as a result you'll rarely see a published story which discusses their existence. Disgusting material, such as detailed descriptions of regurgitations, are taboo for the same reason, as are overdetailed descriptions of surgical operations or mutilations or injuries during fights or accidents. Feeble-mindedness, senility, the birth of abnormal infants, and the mention of excreta are taboo. And, despite the popularity of *The Three Faces of Eve, The Snake Pit,* and others, few editors will touch stories dealing with insanity, particularly where the unpleasant symptoms and results of the mental disease rather than the interesting psychiatric treatment are emphasized.

Stories which deride a particular city or locale, or which boost one political party and slam another, are usually taboo. You'll agree, I think, that it is hard to picture a New Englander enjoying a story which pictures all New Englanders as tight-fisted or mean, or a Democrat enjoying a story wherein all Democrats are depicted as thieves and incompetents and all Republicans as great men. Or vice versa. If you must have a

senator who is a windbag in one of your stories, just neglect
to mention the party to which he belongs. It is also a good
idea to leave out comments against the administration then
current, even if the magazine's editorial page slams the administration all the time.

Stories with excessively trite themes mar reading enjoyment
enough to become taboo, too. You'll have a hard time selling,
for example, stories wherein the chief problem is the paying
off of the mortgage, or wherein the obstacle to the marriage is
the stern father with his inevitable questions about the hero's
financial future, unless you have some absolutely fresh twist.
Editors also tear their hair out these days over stories in which
heroines are described by the trite device of having them look
into mirrors and observe each of their features. (This sort of
thing:

She looked for a long moment in the mirror, admiring her long
taffy-colored hair, her dark eyes, her little upturned nose, and the
way her smooth shoulders shone against the strapless black gown.
She knew the new boy would like her.

Sickeningly familiar, isn't it?)
Other clichés to be avoided, aside from those in the little
example just given, are the nose dusted with freckles, the honey-
or straw-colored hair, and the hero with the crooked or lop-
sided grin. There are many, many more; you know them if you
read a lot.

Themes or types of stories which enjoy a tremendous vogue
eventually slip into the triteness-taboo class. Typical of these
is the reminiscence, or *Life with Father,* type of story, over
which you tripped wherever you turned a while ago, and which
is now rapidly becoming comparatively difficult to sell. There's
a simple method, by the way, of determining whether a category of that type is still okay to write. If, as the months go by,
a story or two of a new type appears, and more and more begin
to appear with each issue, leap onto the bandwagon and get

yours in quickly. If, however, the magazines have been full of this new type for quite a while by the time you spot it, better pass it by; the chances are too good that it will be dead through overuse by the time your story is written and up for sale.

One final reason for the formation of taboos is the fact that, as you are undoubtedly astute enough to realize for yourself, no magazine is as free or unfettered as it would like to be (except possibly the few which do not carry advertising). On the one hand, no outside person can dictate to a magazine editor and tell him what to print and what not to print; on the other hand, you can bet that magazine editors exercise more than reasonable care to avoid offending people who buy advertising space amounting to thousands of dollars a year.

You will have difficulty, obviously, in selling a story in which the hero's new automobile is a lemon and falls to pieces at the crucial moment, since the big slick magazines to which you're offering it run four or five pages of color advertising by automobile manufacturers. It is also easier to push a camel through the eye of a needle than to sell a story about plane crashes to an editor whose magazine carries a lot of airline advertising.

These are general taboos which apply to nearly all magazines and to nearly all kinds of magazines. There are also a number of specific taboos which apply only to specific magazines or to specific story types.

For most Canadian magazines, stories which treat divorce with sympathy or which advocate divorce are taboo, because of Canada's very large Catholic population. The same, of course, applies to stories submitted to Catholic general magazines.

Most women's magazines will pass up stories in which the attitude of the males toward the females is predatory: where, for example, there is considerable description of the way in which the male ogles the female's legs, or admires the tightness of her sweater. They feel that that sort of thing embarrasses their readers.

Both the perfect-crime story—wherein the character plans a perfect murder, and then, at the end, slips up through "one little mistake"—and the biter-bit story—wherein the character plans a perfect murder, and then, through a fluke, falls into the murder trap himself—are now taboo in most magazines using crime fiction. These two types of stories, once among the most popular in the crime field, are additional examples of once very salable forms which became taboos through overuse.

Other taboos in crime stories are those in which the murder happens very late in the story (it should usually happen in the first five pages), narcotics, white slavery, nonmurder stories (almost all crime yarns must be murder stories these days), the clever reporter who solves the crime (once fine, now too trite), the clever rookie cop who solves the crime (same reason), and stories in which the killer escapes without punishment. Another important crime-story taboo is the long-winded explanation after the killer has been exposed; the explanation today must be interspersed in the action in the final capture or exposure scene.

Taboos in Westerns are the overtrite story of the lone cowhand who wanders onto the ranch from which cattle are being rustled, and gets the rancher's daughter and the foreman's job when the foreman turns out to be the thief. You can also add to the same bonfire the hero who sails into a tough situation or cleans up a bad town for no reason other than the interests of justice; he must have a personal stake today. It also, incidentally, isn't cricket or good taste to have a Mexican villain these days, and Indians need not be savage murderers.

Stay away from the rich-boy-whose-college-classmates-think-he's-a-snob-or-wants-to-buy-his-way-onto-the-team-but-he-turns-out-to-be-a-right-guy-in-the-big-game story and the son-who-isn't-quite-as-good-as-his-famous-father story if you write sports yarns, and the poor-gal-who-gets-rich-boss-or-poor-gal-who-is-temporarily-swayed-by-rich-villain-until-she-sees-worth-of-poor-but-honest-hero love stories. These are typical cliché plots, and you can easily recall many others; stay away from them all unless you can work up really fresh twists.

In any type of action story, action for action's sake is no longer desirable. At one time, a specific number of fights or gun battles were usually required, and sometimes the flimsiest of reasons were given to ring these into the yarns. Today, action is still a desirable commodity, but it must be legitimate, unforced action; it must happen because it is the logical thing to happen in the situation stated. It must also, in some way, have a conclusion which advances the story.

No taboo is ever absolute.

As the years pass, stories containing each of the taboos described in the preceding pages will appear in all the leading and smaller magazines. Stories may even appear which contain all the taboos at once. It's easy to understand: irresistibly good stories will continue to be bought, whatever taboos they contain, and bad stories with taboos will continue to find their way into print for the various reasons that bad stories are bought.

Some of the taboos, of course, are designed to keep trite junk out of print, and some—such as the racial-bias taboo—are designed to keep the narrow-minded and the prejudiced from grinding their dirty little axes in public. These are fine; long may they keep in their graves the things they ban. And the good things which are taboo—well, we're moving rapidly in the right direction.

The slick and pulp magazines, once the most timid and least crusading of all publications, are becoming more and more liberal and open-minded all the time, and liberality and open-mindedness always bring with them the understanding that life can be seamy as well as beautiful—and that improvements are possible only when this fact is faced. The realism trend is beginning to point up the fact that, just as there are people in the world who love their wives and never beat them and always bring home fat pay envelopes on Fridays, there are also perverts, and men who cheat on their wives, and people who have venereal diseases, and families who live in broken-down little shacks and never have quite enough to eat. The quality magazines, of course, have always probed deeply. Certainly greater understanding of different problems and different kinds of people will eliminate the necessity for many of the taboos whose only purpose is to avoid and hide the starker realities of life.

Today, however, the taboos are still with us in force, and the new writer who adds the burden of a taboo to his story is like the man who is walking over a narrow and hazardous mountain trail for the first time, and insists on carrying a hundred-pound sack of potatoes under each arm. He would be much wiser, by far, to wait until he knows the trail better, at which time the trail will probably have been widened a little. Then he'll also be equipped to help widen it a bit more.

TWO:
THE STORY-PLANNING
AND PLOTTING FACTS

8

WHERE DO YOU GET YOUR IDEAS?:
Tapping the reservoir

Through the years, a number of mechanical devices have been placed on the market which offer to do your plotting and idea-getting for you. Generally, these work on a system whereby, through selection of cards or the use of a pointer or dial, you come up with one of a choice of heroes, heroines, villains, problems, and so forth. You flip your pointer, or dial your dial, or select your cards, and get something like this:

Hero is a *coal miner*. Heroine is a *movie usherette*. Villain is *mayor of the town*. Problem is (hero and heroine are) *lost in the desert*. Complication is a *flood*. Solution comes about through a *candy bar*.

Probably you can work up a middling fair plot from this conglomeration, and certainly it will test and exercise your ingenuity to figure out how, if your characters' problem is that they are lost in a desert, you can bring a flood into the situation. You will also have to do some mental acrobatics to puzzle out how this battle with the elements is won through the use of a candy bar, or how to give the villain something to do in this story where the troubles clearly come from a Higher Authority. I suppose the villain will have to get the hero and heroine lost in the desert for nefarious reasons of his own, and arrange the flood by loosing some gigantic irrigation system.

These mechanical devices make amusing games, but the fact must be faced that they really are little more than amusing games. They fail as legitimate suppliers of plots and ideas because there is no guarantee that the concoctions they serve up will make *your* kind of story.

Don't misunderstand me: I don't mean that you'll be served a detective story when your preference happens to be family problem stories. Most plotting devices offer different kinds of cards or gadgets for different kinds of stories. The example given, for instance, is a legitimate one, which I worked out before beginning this chapter from a group of cards devoted to adventure stories. The series I used is a simplified one: some of the others give heroes' motives, villains' motives, further complications, and much more.

What I mean is that, within the enormous areas of the general type of story you want to write (family-problem story, light love story, detective story, etc.), there are further considerations which can be determined only by your own particular personality and mental make-up. Perhaps vast and panoramic problems such as floods don't reach your emotions at all; perhaps you are emotionally moved by inner, more basic, problems, such as a man's fears that his wife has stopped loving him because he has taken her away from comfort to the life of a struggling and poverty-stricken farm, or a woman's fears at thirty when she sees that marriage has passed her by. Perhaps you know nothing about miners, or construction engineers, or television repairmen, or the other heroes selected by the plotting devices; perhaps you're interested in the troubles of young farm hands, or the worries of the sweet and lonely girl who works in the store down the street. The best stories you will ever write are those which you understand and feel, the stories which move *you* emotionally just as you hope to move the reader emotionally; and it is an empty hope to expect to achieve exactly the right combination of events and people through the blind, close-your-eyes-and-stick-a-pin approach of mechanical plot devices.

Throughout my experience in the writing business, I have known only three authors who were successful and who used mechanical plot devices for any length of time. And when *they* discovered that, by the time they had twisted and altered the plotting device concoctions to fit their own emotional slant, their stories bore no resemblance to the original concoctions—that, in effect, they had been forming their stories just as though they had not used the plotting devices at all— they discarded them, too. I apologize to the manufacturers of plotting devices for blasting their products in this way, but it is my honest opinion that successful story writing is too emotional and personal a thing to be built on so mechanical a framework.

The same basic flaw exists in all forms of homemade mechanical plotting as well: such as selecting six words at random from the dictionary and using them to build up an idea, or mentally selecting a page number and position in a news magazine and using the news item which appears there, whatever it may be, as the basis for your next story. There is no assurance or promise that these things will fit *your* kind of emotions, or *your* way of thinking, and therefore they're useless to you.

The best way to get story ideas is to draw on your personal experience. You'll need never worry about coming up with the wrong sort of idea, because your own mind and emotions will be doing the work for you. You may conjure up a story idea which fits a field other than your speciality—a detective-story idea may turn up on rare occasions, when your usual field is family-problem stories—but it will always be an idea with which you are emotionally and personally *en rapport*. And, as you gain experience, your mind will school itself to think along the lines of your chosen field, just as it automatically and normally does along the lines of your emotional kind of story.

This personal plotting—this use of yourself as an idea-well—never dries up or gets used up because it is constantly replenished. It grows out of something to which you add every moment of your life: personal experience.

Personal experience is a sort of ambiguous phrase; it is interpreted by too many new writers to mean only the things which have happened to them personally. This is not the sole meaning at all: few of us live a lifetime's worth of story material.

Personal experience, in the idea-getting and story-planning sense, means anything at all which has come under your ken in any way at all. It means things which have happened to you personally, and things which have happened to your relatives and friends and acquaintances, and things about which you've heard in one way or another, and things which you've learned in school, and things about which you're read, or heard on the radio, or seen in the movies or on television. These things are part of your personal experience in the sense that you're aware of them.

If you know a man who is unhappy because his wife is so extravagant that she spends more money on her own clothing than on the upkeep of their children—if you hear about a man who is ruining his life because he can't break the habit of gambling—if you read a story about a man who is miserable because he has been forced into a profession other than the one of his choice—you've added additional story material to your mental file. And nearly everybody runs across that sort of thing a dozen times a week.

This doesn't mean, when you're settling down to write a story, that it will necessarily be about a man whose wife is extravagant, or a man who gambles, or a man who is in the wrong profession. It is the basic causes *behind* these cases which are important to you—the basic factors which cause human troubles.

Your man-in-wrong-job story need not be, for example, about an architect who wishes he were a doctor, if that was the situation in the story you read. The basic factor is maladjustment to circumstances, so your story may be about a timid little bookkeeper who wishes he were an explorer—or, perhaps, an explorer who wishes he had some nice safe job like bookkeeping. (An explorer, of course, would be a poor bet as a character just now—remember the trend toward reader-identification.) The real-life case of the man who gambles may be very sad indeed: but if you write light love stories, and understand the case in its essential ingredient, the fact that people sometimes can't seem to stop themselves from doing things they know are wrong, you can work up an amusing yarn about a man who really loves his fiancée but is in trouble with her because he can't seem to break the habit of turning to admire every pretty girl who passes him on the street.

Every human problem of which you are aware can be transmuted into a dozen different story ideas, or a hundred dozen. The extravagant-woman case can become a very serious story of a man who loves his wife but is torn between two loves when he discovers that she hates their children (perhaps because they've cut down her personal freedom—or perhaps they're his children by a previous marriage); it can become a very humorous story about a man who loves his wife but must cure her of some annoying habit or mannerism, or go mad; it can become the story of a man who resents his wife's extravagance but eventually discovers that he has been selfish in other, more important, ways; it can become the story of a woman who is deliberately extravagant so that her lazy or too easygoing husband will be forced to settle down and work hard to meet the bills; it can become the motive in a crime story. And so on, *ad infinitum*.

This transmutation of everyday occurrences into story ideas, understand, will usually not be a deliberate or conscious process, particularly after you've been working at writing for a while. Few writers actually sit down and say to themselves, "Well, I think I'll shoot one for the slicks this time. Now, what actual occurrence or story I've read would be suitable as a start-off point?" Most of the time, your story ideas will come from springboards deeply imbedded in your subconscious; you'd require the assistance of a team of psychoanalysts to help you trace them back to their initial sources. That is why I say that your storehouse is adding material all the time: with your mind working for you and clicking away every hour of the day, mechanical plotting remains an unnecessary and poor substitute.

You may, of course, have to draw on personal experience consciously at the start, and on those rare later occasions when your subconscious doesn't seem to be functioning right.

Some writers get ideas when they're working on other stories and don't need them, or when they're doing things other than story planning or writing, and then have a devil of a time remembering them or forcing up others when they're ready to begin work on their next scripts. Other writers can usually sit down and work up a good idea any time they need one. If you're in the latter group, you require nothing but congratulations; if you're in the former, get yourself a good, stiff-backed notebook and jot down ideas as they come to you. You can also stick into your notebook any clippings which suggest ideas to you.

Three important tips to notebook users. First, don't note down your ideas in such detail that you feel you've done the thing before when you settle down to write the story, but don't make them too scanty, either. One of my clients once wrote, "Guy needs heebles," in his notebook; he's sure it was a first-class idea, but he's been trying for years to remember what it was. Second, don't keep ideas in your notebook too long without using them: ideas have a way of refreshing themselves over and over again while they're in the back of your mind, but they grow cold and useless when they remain too long in your notebook. And third, don't discuss your ideas. You'll find they'll have lost their excitement or flavor when you get down to writing the stories.

Most writers get their ideas and work out a mental plan of the story before they begin writing; a few sometimes begin writing without an idea at all, and try to develop a story by leading off with a character in trouble or in some unusual situation. This writing-without-a-compass method sometimes works, because the mind swings into action and manages to come forth with a stored-up idea which fits the opening situation, but generally it's bad medicine. You can stack up quite a pile of disjointed and garbled stories that way.

Most of the time, you definitely need a good idea and a plan of action before you begin writing. In the chapters which follow, we're going to discuss the method of building your ideas into salable plots, and take a look at exactly how much prewriting planning is needed.

9

PLOTS THAT SELL: *How to build your ideas into salable stories*

Let's talk about skeletons. One particular skeleton, as a matter of fact: an important little item known as the plot skeleton.

The plot skeleton is my name for it, anyway. Other people have called it the general plot pattern, and the universal plot, and the basic plot structure, and the interior fiction framework, and a couple of dozen other things. Whatever name you give it, it is something which will be completely useless to you if you don't fully understand it—and your best friend in the writing business if you do.

The plot skeleton is the basic structure underlying almost every piece of commercial fiction from fairy tales to classics to the stories in the magazine which will arrive at the corner newsstand on the first of next month. This common denominator runs along these lines:

A sympathetic lead character finds himself in trouble of some kind, and makes active efforts to get himself out of it. Each effort, however, merely gets him deeper into his trouble, and each new obstacle in his path is larger than the last. Finally, when things look blackest, and it seems certain that the lead character is kaput, he manages to get out of his trouble through his own efforts, intelligence, or ingenuity.

Now let's make a simple test. Can you think of lots of stories which are not built around the plot skeleton as described? Do you believe that only a small portion of published stories *are* built around the plot skeleton as described? That's our test—for, if so, you have indicated that you don't really understand the plot skeleton as fully as you should.

What you are forgetting, as so many people do, is that the plot skeleton *is* a skeleton—and that it may look so different with one layer of outer flesh than with another that it is hard to believe that the two are identical inside. Remember that, when you take two identical female skeletons and cover them differently, one is Marjorie Main, and the other is Marilyn Monroe. They are still, however, identical in skeletal structure.

The plot skeleton in its simplest or most obvious form— which is the one many inexperienced writers assume all plot skeleton stories to be—is the one where the lead character gets into trouble which is big, surface, and physical: let us say, by way of example, that he is framed for a murder. He makes an active physical effort to get out of trouble—let us say he sneaks up into the murder room to examine the evidence and see if he can find some clue to the real killer—and the way this deepens his trouble is also surface and obvious to all who read the story: the cops enter the room suddenly and, though he manages to elude them and escape, they're surer than ever that he's guilty because they assume he came up there to destroy the evidence against *him*.

Then he makes another physical effort to get out of his trouble—he sneaks over to see the chief witness in the hope that he can get the truth out of her—and again the further deepening of his trouble is obvious: he's a little rough about it in his eagerness, and she believes (or pretends to believe) that he's trying to kill her, and she screams and he runs away, and when the police come she says he's certainly the murderer because he just tried to kill her to shut her up. Some more physical efforts to clear himself—some more unexpected results which make him look guiltier than ever—and then, when things look blackest and he's just about strapped in the electric chair, he works out something through his own intelligence, efforts, or ingenuity which enables him to trap or unmask the real murderer and clear himself.

You don't need a strong magnifying glass to see the plot skeleton in that story; its bones stick out along the surface every inch of the way. You can take a pencil and encircle each ingredient as it turns up in the story: the trouble—the efforts to overcome the trouble—the deepening of the trouble with each effort—the reaching of the peak-point of despair— followed by the solution through the lead character's own efforts. The story is a perfectly salable example of the basic plot skeleton structure in fiction, but it is not the only one.

Let's have a look at another example: a light love story wherein the boy and girl fall in love and then become estranged due to a fight or a misunderstanding. They still love each other, of course, and the boy makes a number of efforts to win the girl back—but, sadly enough, estranges her further with each effort. And then, finally, he manages to succeed in winning her back, and they live, let us hope, happily ever after.

Here the plot skeleton is a little deeper below the surface, but it is still not too far hidden. The trouble is not physical danger, as in the previous example, but it is still trouble: the hero may lose forever the girl he loves. He makes definite efforts to overcome his trouble and win the girl back, and just as definitely kicks the goal further away than ever in doing so. And finally, when things are blackest and it seems certain that the romance will never resume, the hero succeeds in overcoming his trouble and winning the girl back. A number of people, however, will solemnly list this light love story as an example of one which does not contain the plot skeleton structure.

Let's take one more story: one about a man who has grown

rather used to his wife and fancies himself in love with a slick young chick who works in his office. He manages to anesthetize his conscience a little, and rationalize his actions—despite an inner, gnawing feeling of guilt—by blaming the marital breakup on his wife's coldness, or something of that sort. But at the end, for any one of a variety of reasons, he has come to know that his wife is best for him, and he goes back to her.

There may be no physical action of any kind in this story: it may even be, throughout, a story of a struggle in a man's mind. When it is well done, the plot skeleton is not visible to the inexpert or semi-expert eye at all, but it is built on a plot skeleton structure just as definitely as the other examples. It is a plot skeleton in every way: there is trouble—the man's indecision between his wife and the young girl; his efforts to solve it are his mental churning and the battle between his rationalization and the feeling of guilt; it grows blacker because his mental struggles and strife make him less and less able to decide which choice is the right one; and the trouble is beaten when he makes the right choice and goes back to his wife.

You've taken five giant steps in the direction of intelligent story planning when you understand that the plot skeleton is not just a formula for one kind of story—that it is not a formula at all, but, rather, a listing of the basic ingredients which go into the making of nearly all fiction of all types. A fiction formula is a restricting affair which shows you how to do a specific kind of story in a specific way; the plot skeleton names the basic ingredients and then allows you to mold and use them in any way you see fit. To assume that stories must be routine or along a single trail because they contain specific basic ingredients is to assume that all cakes must be alike because they all contain flour and sugar, or that all stories must be the same because they're all made up of words and punctuation marks.

You'll find it impossible, I think, to detect external resemblances between the crime story described in this chapter and that great character study and modern classic, *Goodbye, Mr. Chips*—yet both contain the same internal structure. Analyze the Hilton story, and you'll see that it is about a man with a problem (the fear that he'll fail at the work which means his entire life to him—teaching), who makes active efforts to overcome the problem (by being hard and stern because he believes these are the qualities most required in a good teacher), but whose continued efforts only make the problem blacker (he fails more and more as a teacher because the students hate him for his sternness), and who finally solves his problem by becoming, through the example of his sweet and gentle wife, kind and understanding to his students—and thereby a great and beloved teacher.

Nor, among the infinite variety of stories built around the plot skeleton, must the lead character always be aware of his problem at the start, or always solve it happily. Sydney Carton, in *A Tale of Two Cities,* for example, resolves the problem of his weakness of character by doing "a far, far better thing" than he has ever done before—he gives his life for the happiness and safety of others. In some stories, as a matter of fact, the solution need not even be certain: the story may end on the note that there is hope for happiness at last, or that it looks as though everything is going to be all right.

One other variation is the inverted plot skeleton, the exact opposite of the standard plot skeleton. In the regular plot skeleton story, attention is focused on a sympathetic lead character, and reader interest is built up through the fear that he may not succeed in solving his problem—until, at the end, he does. In the inverted skeleton story, the lead character is an unsympathetic person who succeeds more and more in his evil doings, and reader interest is held through the fear that he'll succeed completely—until, at the end, he fails.

The best way to understand the reason for the plot skeleton is to examine its make-up.

The reason for the need of a definitely sympathetic or unsympathetic lead character is a simple one: if your reader doesn't care much about your lead—if he neither likes nor dislikes him particularly—he isn't going to be much interested in what happens to him. You've got to make absolutely sure that your reader is cheering or jeering your lead if you want him to remain interested all the way through.

You can see the reason for the basic problem, of course: a smooth-running life is pleasant to watch, but it doesn't grip a reader's interest for long. The moment a character he likes gets into trouble, however, it's another thing again—he's right alongside, rooting for him all the way. And that, too, is the reason for the complications—the constant sinking deeper and deeper in the pit, the constantly larger and larger rocks in the path to safety. If a problem looks easy to solve, why worry about it?

And when things have reached their lowest ebb, when the black clouds are thickest, and the hero finally manages to solve his problem—he's got to do it himself. As you can understand, it's pretty frustrating to watch an admirable character struggle and struggle against obstacles: and then, at the end, see somebody else get him out of the jam. You're more than a little disappointed in the man, and you also feel cheated. Keep the fortuitous arrival of the U.S. Marines out of your stories; if your character's worthy of being the lead in your story, he should be man enough to do all the final problem solving personally. There have been some pretty fair stories in which someone other than the lead solves the problem at the end, but they would have been infinitely more satisfying if the lead had done the job himself.

When you've got a good idea for a story—which is usually just another way of saying that you've worked up a strong and fresh problem and a strong and fresh solution—use the plot skeleton to work out the details, and then use it as a yard-stick to see that everything is okay. If all the bones are strong, and all the bones are there, you won't ever have to worry about having a sick plot.

10

WHEN IS A STORY NOT A STORY?: *Incident* vs. *story*

Let's see if we can work up a quick freehand definition of a story on the basis of the discussion of plotting in the preceding chapter. It would probably run something like this:

A story is a description of events stemming from a problem and eventually resulting in resolution of that problem. To put it another way, it is what happens when someone has a problem and overcomes it.

I've stated it simply and basically because I want you to note one particular thing: a story follows a straight and well-defined line from beginning to end. In a nutshell, it moves from the basic problem (whether it is a struggle against visible trouble or a man's strife within his own mind or what have you) directly to the resolution of that problem (whether it is happy or unhappy or definite or just hopeful for the future or what have you). There are boulders in the path—the difficulties in solving the problem which build up suspense and nail the reader to his chair—but it is a straight path leading to a definite and desired-by-the-reader destination.

That is a story. Now let's see if we can work up a definition of an incident:

An incident is a description of an event or series of events, and nothing more. It does not necessarily go anywhere or make any definite point.

The difference between the two, in other words, is that the

first describes events with a definite reason for doing so—the events are moving the story toward the solution of a conundrum established at the beginning; the other describes an event or events for the mere sake of describing them.

The presence of urgency-to-reach-a-particular-destination in a story and its absence in an incident is the reason for the fact that a story is salable and an incident is not. A story holds the reader's interest and keeps him interested throughout; an incident merely tells him about something in which there's no reason or necessity for him to be interested at all.

A great many new writers, for example, believe they are writing a salable story when they tell the tale of a boy and girl who meet in an office and like each other and decide to get married. This isn't a story at all; it is something you tell in a letter to someone who knows the boy and girl and therefore has a personal reason for being interested. It is of no interest to the reader of fiction because it follows a routine course and contains nothing to worry him and grip his attention. Even if they meet in an unusual way and fall in love in an unusual way and the marriage ceremony is performed while they're standing on their heads on a plane wing, nothing more is achieved than a casual and fleeting interest at each unusual occurrence— because the story lacks the *sustained* attention-grip which comes with never-lessening worry over a strong problem and whether or not it can be overcome.

You have a *story* when the boy and girl break up for some reason—when a basic problem arises—and when their efforts to get together just drive them further apart (the complications)—and when it finally looks as though they'll never get together (the things-look-darkest point)—and when they finally *do* get together. The reader can sigh with relief at *this* conclusion because he has had his vicarious thrill of worrying over whether or not they would get together at all. Naturally, he sort of knew that they would get together at the end, but the increasing blackness of the storm clouds gave him a you-never-can-tell feeling which is completely lacking in the untroubled and foregone-conclusion incident.

The incident, for that matter, could even have ended with the characters deciding not to get married after all, and the reader wouldn't have cared particularly. It's just too late when you wait until the end of a story to remember that a reader must worry to enjoy. You've given him no reason to worry that things may go wrong—all you've done is told the dull and placid story of a dull and placid courtship—so what the devil is it to him if you decide at the end to have the boy and girl split up?

The vital factor, in fiction, of a problem and the hard fight to overcome it and its eventual overcoming has been given a great many technical names. The one which describes the necessity of moving steadily toward a definite destination is frequently called story-line delineation; the one which describes the struggles in overcoming it is frequently called conflict. Whatever the names, however, you just can't do without it.

The conflict may be outward—as in a struggle of man against man, or man against circumstances or events—and it may be inward—as in a man's mental struggle against himself—but it must be there. A story without struggle is no story at all.

Undoubtedly, many writers turn out incidents because they're unaware of these facts and believe they are writing stories; others do so deliberately because they have seen some very fine pieces published which they believe *are* only incidents. These writers would do well to look again. A story like the one about the man who's too used to his wife and falls for a young girl but at the end decides to return to his wife, for example, might easily appear to be an incident, particularly since there is little external action and it all may take place in one scene. It is not an incident, however; it is a complete and satisfying story because it contains all the necessary elements of the problem and the struggle to overcome it and its final overcoming.

You'll find this to be true as well of almost all other published stories which may at first appear to be nothing more than incidents. The characters may even do nothing but sit around and talk from the first line to the last, but there is a definite *direction* in the things they are saying—a special undertone in the conversation which moves inevitably toward the resolution of the basic problem. Even ultraliterary stories move from a basic problem to an ultimate resolution of the problem: though here, in the field where sorrow so often reigns supreme, the resolution is often that You Can't Win and the character had better learn to suffer in silence.

An incident, you must also keep in mind, can only be made into a story by the addition of a basic problem and movement toward solution; never simply by the addition of more incidents, as some people suppose. This illusion probably arises from unawareness of the difference between the dictionary definition of the word and its meaning in fiction writing.

The dictionary defines an incident as a single event or happening; the fiction field defines it as an isolated or self-contained occurrence of any kind—in the sense that it is just "a piece" and not a full story line. The typical incident example given—boy and girl meet and like each other and decide to get married—would, for instance, be only a small part of an acceptable story: probably just the occurrence before they break up and the problem starts.

In other words, a script doesn't avoid being an incident merely because it covers a number of scenes rather than just one: if the whole thing sums up as a problemless and conflictless occurrence, it is an unsalable incident even if it takes a hundred scenes to tell. Boy-and-girl-meet-and-like-each-other-and-decide-to-get-married misses because it lacks suspense and the factors which grip and hold a reader's attention; it doesn't become any more suspenseful and reader-gripping if the boy and girl meet and begin to like each other in Scene One, meet at the same place the next day and like each other some more in Scene Two, go dancing together and like each other some more in Scene Three, decide to become engaged in Scene Four, get together and arrange for the wedding in Scene Five, and so on and so on and so on *ad nauseam.*

It doesn't even help if they have a little tiff in Scene Six and make up in Scene Seven, and another little tiff and reunion in Scenes Eleven and Twelve, because these are little pebbles which hardly mar the walk up Lovers' Lane. You get your reader and hold him only by bringing your problem onstage early and making it darker and darker as you go along. That basic problem is a big boulder blocking the road, the subsequent complications make it even bigger, and when the problem reaches its crisis—when things look blackest—it is a mile high. A few scattered pebbles just aren't in the same league.

Some more huzzahs for the plot skeleton, in conclusion, because you'll always write a complete story if you follow it carefully. We'll put each of its bones under a microscope in the next few chapters.

11

THE BIG HEADACHE: *The problem*

Two simple words are your best yardsticks for measuring the strength of your story problems. Mark them down: *must* and *cannot*.

The lack of one or the other of these, or both of them, is the chief reason for the rejection of so many stories on the grounds of weakness of the basic problem. It is the chief reason that so many stories are rejected as "too slight," for editors usually use this phrase to cover any story in which the basic problem and its resulting events just don't seem adequate to retain the readers' interest.

Some examples will illustrate this.

Let's say that you have a character named Jimmy Jones who wakes up one morning and decides that he's finally going to buy a one-family house, a thing he's dreamed of doing for many years. He leaps into his trousers and washes and shaves and finishes dressing and breakfasts hurriedly, and the rest of the script follows him as he looks at various unsuitable houses, and then finds a good one and buys it.

Strictly speaking, Jones has a problem: the finding and buying of a suitable one-family house. For fiction purposes, however, it just isn't enough, for his problem lacks the *must* ingredient—an urgency or pressing necessity to find and buy the house. Since he won't be in trouble or any the worse off if he doesn't find and buy one, the reader has no strong reason to worry over or be interested in his search.

All right, you correct it. You have Jones awakened by a phone call from an attorney, who tells him that Ebenezer Jones, his eccentric great-uncle, has just passed on. Under the terms of Ebenezer's will, young Jimmy will inherit a vast fortune (which will, incidentally, enable him to get Mrs. Jimmy the fantastically expensive medical treatment required to save her life, which he cannot afford otherwise), provided he manages to own and live in a one-family house that next night. Jimmy yanks out his savings—enough to buy a house, though not to pay for the treatments—and rushes off and buys one, thereby winning through to the vast fortune.

Now you're closer, for he has a definite and urgent reason that he *must* get that house—but you're still not there. However urgent a problem may be, it still isn't worrisome if it can be easily solved. And Jimmy's can, of course, because all he has to do is rush out and buy a house. The ingredient of *cannot* is lacking.

You get your genuinely strong and adequate problem if Ebenezer made his fortune by building green one-family houses with red gables, and insists, for sentimental reasons, that the house his heir must own be a green one with red gables—and there just aren't any of that description close enough (even by plane) for Jimmy to reach and buy and live in, all by that night. You've got a problem with a must—Jimmy *must* find that house because he needs the vast fortune to save his wife's life—and it seems that he *cannot* find it, because there aren't any of that sort around. If Jimmy is a sympathetic and likable lead character, you'll have little trouble keeping your reader around to watch him fight to solve this worrisome problem.

I've poked a little fun at trite plotting with this example, of course—odd wills and wives-who-need-operations-immediately have been done to death—but I think the point is clear.

If your problem lacks urgency, or if it can be easily solved, it isn't doing properly or fully the job for which it has been set up: to worry the reader over its outcome. You must never make the mistake of assuming that your reader will automatically be interested in your story.

You've got to remember that your reader is a human being with troubles and concerns of his own, and his attention will lag if you don't pull him quickly out of his own world into the world of your story. You do it best when you give him the kind of problem which could conceivably confront *him*, because that establishes reader-identification, but it must be a problem so interestingly urgent and apparently insoluble that it defeats his natural tendency to give his attention to his own concerns.

This does not mean, obviously, that every problem you choose in writing your stories must be a life-or-death affair; it means that, within the limits of the kind of story you're writing, you've got to make the problem so logically worrisome to the lead character that the reader will begin to worry along in sympathy. In the light love story, for example, the reader doesn't expect or require dire circumstances or disaster, but the hero's desire to get the girl must still be made urgent and important enough—despite the humorous circumstances which keep them apart—that the reader will remain intensely interested in their efforts to get together.

It's those two all-important ingredients at work again: must and cannot. For, despite the relative unimportance of the boy-wants-girl-he's-recently-met problem compared to, let us say, one involving a man's struggle to save his life, the successful light love story becomes important by convincing the reader that the boy *must* have that girl, and, for one reason or another, it seems that he *cannot*.

Another thing you must remember is that urgency of problem means immediacy as well as importance to the lead character. As a result, an important-to-the-hero and apparently unsoluble problem will be inadequate, too, if it is something which occurs again and again and has no special reason for immediate solution as your story opens. An example might be a farmer's year-after-year battle against locusts. This problem may certainly be important to him to solve, because it's ruining his farm, and it may be apparently insoluble because he just can't seem to get rid of the pests, but it lacks adequate urgency because he has been fighting the locusts for years and may be doing so for years longer. It would become an urgent problem only if the locusts were arriving for the first time, and he had to get rid of them at once or watch his crop ruined in a matter of hours or days; or if they had been coming for years and his farm was almost barren, and, as the story opened, they were coming again and he had to get rid of them at once this time or be ruined completely. In both cases, of course, to complete the urgency, he'd make strong but unsuccessful efforts to get rid of them—and manage it only when things looked blackest.

Generally, job and money problems fall into the same category: they usually aren't adequate by themselves. If the lead is struggling to get money—let's say a particular sum of money, such as a cash first prize in a contest—just for the sake of getting money, it isn't sufficient because there's no real urgency or pressing necessity for that money, and no real trouble if he doesn't get it. If the lead is struggling to keep his job just for the sake of keeping his job, it fails because the reader's casual reaction is that he can always get another job if he loses this one, particularly these days. There must, therefore, be a special and urgent need for that money—anything but the old wife-needs-an-expensive-operation-immediately, please—or a particular and urgent reason that he must keep the job.

Sometimes, a problem with inadequate urgency can be made adequately urgent if it is tied in with a psychological characteristic of your lead, or some other psychological factor. The problem of a man who may lose his job and who is struggling to keep it just for the sake of keeping it is not, as I have said, usually an adequate one, but it becomes an adequate one if, for example, the lead character has lost a number of jobs in the recent past and will lose the last fragments of his self-confidence and self-respect if he is dropped from *this* job. If well done, the problem has actually been altered from the weak one of a man struggling to keep his job to the strong one of a man struggling to retain his mental balance.

Another example might be the story of a boy who wants a dog but is opposed by his parents and guardians, a yarn you see quite often in adult magazines despite the general editorial tendency away from child-viewpoint stories in this field. Hundreds of new writers turn out very fresh variations on this theme, but find their stories are rejected because the problem isn't strong enough. (The boy really wouldn't be too much the worse off if he didn't get the dog.) The difference between these stories and most of the accepted yarns is that the latter usually add a psychological factor: the boy, for example, is an orphan living with cold and unaffectionate foster parents, and, the reader realizes, he *must* have the dog to fill his psychological need for love and affection.

Almost any problem becomes strong enough with *must* and *cannot* ingredients added, through psychological angles or any other. Even our old pal Jimmy Jones could get by with hunting his one-family house just to get a one-family house if the story should show believably and sympathetically that the hope for this house had been his one dream in life, and that, for some reason, he must get it now or never.

One of the most apt descriptive titles ever given an illness—in this case a story illness—is the "paper dragon." Its name explains it: a paper dragon is a monster which looks real and fearsome at first, but which turns out, on closer examination, only to be made of paper.

The paper-dragon story is one in which the lead character believes he has a serious problem, and spends the entire story trying to overcome that problem, only to discover at the end that the problem never existed at all. A typical paper-dragon story might be one in which a woman decides that her husband doesn't love her any more, goes through all sorts of emotional and mental travail in her efforts to right the situation, and then discovers at the end that he *does* love her after all—that the only reason he didn't get her the birthday present was that he had to save up one more day's subway fare to buy that $60,000 chinchilla coat.

You don't need a crystal ball to imagine the average reader's reaction to that sort of thing. Here he has sweated along with the heroine all through the story under the assumption that she had a serious problem—here he was wasting all that sympathy—and it turns out that she had no problem at all, except perhaps her jackass tendency to jump to conclusions. Editors, of course, spare their readers this reaction by bouncing paper-dragon stories as rapidly as they spot them.

Let me state this in a throbbing, pleading voice: when you give your reader a strong problem to worry over, make sure it remains a strong problem which the lead character manages to resolve at the end. Don't let it turn out to be one of those gee-I-was-wrong-I've-no-problem-after-all affairs, or I make no guarantee for your personal safety if one slips into print. It isn't a hard mistake to make, either, so watch it.

Blood relative to the paper-dragon story is the "idiot plot," also called the "Hollywood plot," because of the movie colony's supposed partiality to it. It gets its name from the fact that the only thing which keeps the problem from being resolved almost at the start is that the characters act like idiots in order to keep the plot moving.

In the idiot-plot story, for example, the hero, a doughnut salesman, misses a date with the heroine because his employer has sent him suddenly out of town to line up a big doughnut eater in Poughkeepsie. The heroine automatically assumes, for no discernible reason, that the hero was out with some girl, so she rushes off to her grandmother's home to be consoled. The hero, returning and rushing to see the girl to apologize and tell her of the big order he's snagged, finds her away and, without discernible reason, assumes she is away with some man, and goes off to *his* grandmother to be consoled. Later they meet and, proudly, tell each other that they had been out on dates those days. ("If she thinks that, by gosh, I'll let her think so!" "If he thinks that, by glory, I'll let him think so!")

By all the rules of logic, in other words, their spat would have been settled in three minutes if they had acted like normal human beings at any of the several opportunities presented and made the simple explanations necessary. Instead, they act in just the opposite manner, with the only possible reason being that if they did explain, the story would be over. In some idiot-plot yarns, their adriotness at doing the illogical thing is truly remarkable.

The *cannot* ingredient must be legitimate: the strong problem will hold up only if the lead character cannot solve it however hard he tries. If he misses solving the problem early in the game only because of his own stupidity, or by missing opportunities a man in his position would not logically miss, the answer is that you haven't a strong, apparently insoluble problem. He must be defeated in his efforts to solve the problem because *anybody* would be defeated.

One more problem pitfall is the "white elephant," wherein the lead character struggles through the first half of the story to get something—and then discovers that he doesn't want it after all, and struggles through the second half to get rid of it. If a problem is worth struggling to solve at all, the solution must bring worth-while and satisfactory results. The white-elephant story also defeats its own purpose, because it reveals that, if the thing the lead struggles to get turns out to be unneeded, there was no real urgency behind his struggles in the first place: he was just foolish in thinking there was.

And one last problem to avoid is the borrowed-trouble variety, which occurs in the hero-sticks-his-snoot-in-somebody-else's-business story. This is the one wherein, in its worst examples, the hero just barges into some situation which is no business of his at all, and bustles around for the rest of the story solving some problem in which he has no personal stake. (For example, a newspaper reporter hero is sent to get the story on a body found in a hotel room, and spends the rest of the yarn running around acting like a cop and trying to solve the murder—ignoring his newspaper job so completely that he never even phones in details of developments.) In its slightly less terrible examples, it is the one in which the hero has some acquaintance who is in trouble, and goes to work to get him out of it.

In any of its examples, this sort of story is not as satisfying, or anywhere nearly as salable, as the story in which the problem is the lead character's own, and he struggles to solve it because it is personally necessary that he do so. The reader's attention is held in fiction because he is made to feel sympathetic toward the lead character, and he is, therefore, interested in watching him solve the strong problem which confronts him. His interest will be greatly lessened, and often even dissolved entirely, if the problem turns out to be someone else's altogether.

A story may be acceptable if the lead character works to get his fiancée, or his wife, or his kid brother, or his best friend, out of a jam, because that really isn't borrowed trouble: if it is established that he loves the person very much, the person's troubles are almost his. Otherwise, the vogue for the I-do-it-because-I'm-interested-in-people story (of which a few examples, such as the Scattergood Baines stories, still survive—

although Scattergood usually manages to achieve some personal gain while he's helping others) has passed. Ninety-nine
out of a hundred borrowed-trouble stories would be enormously
improved if the helping-hand lead were heaved out entirely,
and the person in trouble made the lead, with the problem to
overcome for himself.

12

HIT HIM WHEN HE'S DOWN: *Complications*

Hollywood is going to do a little work for us in this chapter. It's going to provide an example of a hero whose problem complications are so good that they aren't any good at all.

All this happens in a picture, of course: one in which the hero is a man who has been arrested and convicted for a murder he did not commit. Later, he is helped to escape from prison by the heroine, who feels sympathy toward him because her father had died in prison following conviction for a crime *he* did not commit, either. The hero returns to his old neighborhood to try to clear himself by finding the real murderer.

After several attempts, during which the police grow hotter and hotter on his trail, and things look blacker and blacker, he succeeds: he discovers and confronts the real murderer, an older woman. She admits it calmly, pointing out, however, that he can be cleared only if she is around to be made to confess publicly. And then, before he can stop her, she underlines her hatred for him by leaping out of a window to her death.

I remember feeling considerable admiration for the script writers at this point. "Here," I thought, "is complication-upon-complication-to-reach-blackest-point-of-despair at its best. Now the hero *really* seems to be sunk. I wonder how he's going to get out of it."

And then my admiration broke into little pieces, because he just didn't. He shrugged his shoulders in despair, and the final scene showed the hero and heroine happily meeting by arrangement in a South American country where extradition is not permitted.

The movie, in short, had settled for a plain, garden-variety insult to the intelligence. It expected the audience to believe that a man of the hero's strength of character and determination could happily and contentedly live the rest of his life away from the country of his birth, forever in exile for a crime he knew he had not committed.

What the writers had done, technique-wise, was overshoot their mark. They had worked so hard to make the problem complications blacker and blacker and apparently insoluble that they had made it really insoluble. And so they had been forced to fall back on a solution which could not fail to dissatisfy, particularly in view of the fact that the rest of the picture had been devoted to the hero's gigantic efforts to clear himself. He could, after all, have gone to the South American country right after his escape, His problem was to clear himself, not to avoid recapture, and that problem remained unsolved at the picture's end.

The purpose of complications in your stories, as we have discussed, is to increase and continue to increase the worriment which you set up in the reader when you first show him the problem confronting the sympathetic lead character. Its purpose is also to increase his desire to see the problem solved and to frustrate the desire with each new and greater complication until you fulfill it at the end of the story. You must, therefore, make sure that the complications are sufficiently black to build up that worriment and desire but not so black that you find yourself unable at the end to furnish the lead with the relief he deserves.

The killer's suicide in the picture was an error of technique because it did actually shut off the hero's last avenue of solution of his problem: it would have been perfectly acceptable if it had only *seemed* to shut off that last avenue, because it sunk the hero and the audience in the necessary deepest depth of despair. If the hero had managed to solve his problem despite that final kick in the heart, the film would have been an entirely satisfactory one instead of a quite good one which fell apart at the end.

When you plan your problem and complications, it is usually safest to plan your solution at the same time. If you just go ahead and write your story up through the final complication, without knowing how you're going to end it, you're liable to find yourself just as puzzled about a logical solution as your lead character. And then, as in the picture just described, you may be strongly tempted to conclude with a weakish device, and that isn't good. Your reader will never be satisfied if the big firecracker you've built up goes off with a bang as loud as a sheet of paper dropped on a thick rug.

Complications are like sunbaths: they miss their purpose if each new one doesn't make things a little darker.

Every complication faces the danger of being nothing more than an out-and-out irritant to the reader. All complications are irritants, in a way, because they keep the reader temporarily from seeing what he wants to see: the lead character solve the problem. Complications which rise out of the lead's efforts to solve the problem, and which make the situation look blacker, have a definite purpose—the stronger the pain, the sweeter the relief—and you can get away with them because the hero is doing what the reader wants him to do (struggling to solve the problem) and the complications are logical, if unfortunate, results. But when a complication occurs "on the side"—when it does not result from the hero's direct efforts to solve his problem—it accomplishes nothing more than to delay the story movement and cut its suspense; and it irritates the reader without any compensating factors whatever.

Take, for example, the familiar complication which occurs when the lead character is speeding along in a car with the gas pedal down to the floor, because it is vital to the solution of the problem that he reach a particular place at a particular time—and suddenly he is halted at a railroad crossing while a long freight train moves slowly and agonizingly past. This is a legitimate complication because it does make things look blacker—the lead will fail to overcome his problem if he doesn't reach that certain place on time. On the other hand, if it doesn't matter whether he gets there in a few minutes or a few hours, the freight-train incident should not be used as a complication at all—because it becomes pointless. Without a time limit coupled to the basic problem, it doesn't affect the problem in any way, or make things look blacker; all it does is slow down, or stop, the story.

Because many writers don't actually realize that the only purpose of complications is to increase suspense by making the solution possibilities appear darker and darker, the use of the unsatisfactory complication—to give it a name: the reasonless complication—is a common error. When the lead character must see another character as a possibility of solving his problem in the reasonless-complication stories, the other character is always away or hard to find at first. Actually, this doesn't accomplish a thing toward the building of suspense: on the contrary, it is only the meeting with the other character and the discovery that the interview with him doesn't help solve the problem that makes the solution possibilities look blacker. And when the lead must go somewhere, transportation is always slow or difficult to find—which is exactly the wrong tack, because it is only when the lead gets there and is unsuccessful in his solution attempt that the problem grows grimmer.

Be careful about those complications of yours. Weigh each

one painstakingly before you use it. And, if you find that it only delays matters a little instead of making things materially worse, don't use it at all. It will only do your story more harm than good.

Most reasonless complications also suffer from the fact that they are coincidental—and however often coincidences may occur in real life, they always manage to look phony when they turn up in fiction. You may have just finished drinking two quarts of water the first time anyone ever offered to buy you an ice-cream soda, come down with mumps the day you were supposed to go to the first party in your life at which you were sure there'd be kissing games, and tripped and broken your hipbone as you were rushing from the church with your new mate to go to the honeymoon hotel; but throw these globs of bad luck at a lead character in a story, and the public will find them difficult to swallow. You can get by with an occasional bit of coincidence such as the passing-freight-train complication—it is, of course, a bit coincidental that the train just happened to be passing at the moment the hero just happened to pass that point at a time when he just happened to be in a terrific hurry—but you can keep coincidence from showing up too often by making sure that almost all of your complications occur because they're the only things which *could* logically occur as the result of the lead character's unsuccessful efforts to solve his problem.

Another way to avoid the boring and the movement stopping in your complications is to be careful that your problem does not suggest an enormous number of solution possibilities. This error usually results in the kind of story wherein the problem is not too difficult, but the lead just can't seem to get it solved no matter how hard he tries. He sees one person after another and does one thing after another—all to no avail.

First of all, you're violating a basic rule of problem choosing when you select one of this sort, because the problem must look insoluble to grip the reader's attention at all—and he won't wait around long enough for the complications to start if the basic problem looks as though it will be a cinch to solve. And secondly, complications on the same level of suspense can grow mighty boring; there's just nothing exciting about one failure to solve after another.

Anything can grow tedious through repetition: even a fight to the death, if the same action occurs over and over again. (Hero and villain fight at cliff's edge overlooking ocean, and villain pushes hero over; hero parts the water neatly, swims out, rejoins the villain and fights some more, and the villain pushes him over again; again he swims out and fights some more with the villain, and again the villain pushes him over; and one more swim-out, fight, and dunking. After several of these forcible dunkings, the hero's soaking wet, the villain's shoulders ache from pushing—and the reader's asleep.) The suspense, therefore, must mount steadily: the basic problem should look absolutely insoluble, only one solution possibility should occur at a time, each attempt to solve the problem should be a strong struggle, and each failure to do so should make the problem seem all the harder to solve.

Make use of your limits when planning your complications: the time limit ("If I don't find the document by nine o'clock, I'm lost"), and the solution-possibilities limit ("If *this* doesn't win Jane back, I'm sunk"). Limits make things more difficult for your lead character, and that is your job in the fiction business.

13

THE FINAL SANDBAG: *The crisis-point*

One of the staff editors at my agency defines the problem as the first heavy sandbag which hits the lead character and knocks him to the ground, the complications as additional sandbags which pin him more and more tightly to the ground, and the crisis as the time when one final sandbag completes the pinning down so thoroughly that it seems certain he can never get out from under.

Each new complication in a story makes the situation blacker, but there is always, when the lead recovers a little from the shock of the new complication and peers into the darkness, a faint ray of light and hope—something else he can try which may solve his problem. The sandbags are heavy on his back, but he can still, perhaps, flex his muscles and force his way out. The final complication which brings on the crisis, however, comes when the *last* attempt fails: the time when "this is my last chance—if it misses, I'm finished," and it misses.

It is the time, in the man-*vs.*-the-elements-or-environment story, when the farmer uses the last possible object which may rid his acreage of the locusts, and it doesn't succeed and his farm is doomed. It is the time, in the man-*vs.*-man story, when the hero exhausts or loses his last weapon, and the heavily armed villain moves in for the inevitable kill. It is the time, in the man-*vs.*-himself story, when he knows certainly that he cannot overcome his weakness, or when he makes the final and irrevocable wrong decision or choice. It is, in any kind of story, the highest peak-point of suspense for the reader, because it is the moment of greatest certainty of absolute failure for the sympathetic lead character or (in the reverse skeleton) the moment of greatest certainty of absolute success for the unsympathetic lead character.

Naturally, the certainty is not as certain as all that. The farm is not really lost—death at the villain's hands is not really inevitable—the wrong choice is not really irrevocable, as the eventual solution shows. It does, however, *seem* absolutely certain at the crisis-point, until the final event in the story comes along; whereas after each earlier complication it merely seemed extremely likely.

Plot construction, considered in that way, is a sort of carefully managed, increasingly loud crying of wolf by the author, with the wolf being the impossibility of solving the problem. Actually the wolf is never there, for the problem *is* solved at the end: but, until the end, the reader is made to believe it is there by the apparent insolubility of the basic problem and by the way the added complications seem to prove that the problem is insoluble. And, fortunately for the writing business, readers—unlike the shepherds in the fable—never fail to show up because of all the previous wolf crying; a good new story with a fresh problem and fresh complications will start them worrying about the wolf all over again.

Just as the job of the problem and complications is to make the reader feel that solution is very likely impossible, the job of the crisis is to make him feel *certain* that it is impossible. A new depth of despair, rock bottom, is reached; his worry sinks from, "My gosh, this thing may beat the lead character," to "My God, it has!" Things may have looked bad previously, but at least there was always some possibility to be tried; now things look absolutely terrible, and it seems as though all possibilities are exhausted. With your crisis, you give the reader the ultimate in pain, which makes his relief all the more pleasant when the lead character uncovers one more unexpected avenue and wins through to success.

Remember that differentiation between earlier complications and the crisis. After each of the lead character's efforts end unsuccessfully, and result in complications and general darkening of the situation, he may have to think a bit and then come up with another possibility to try, or he may locate and try another possibility almost immediately. At the crisis-point, however, there must seem to be no other possibilities left, and therefore the struggle of conjuring up the final possibility and solving the problem must be the strongest struggle in the entire story. It is always a good idea to have each new possibility come hard to the lead character, because it builds suspense—though don't confuse this with the error of delays which keep the lead from coming to grips with the possibility once he thinks of it— but the last one must come hardest of all.

The story, in other words, must actually *reach* a point where no possibilities are evident, and where the final possibility which causes the solution is pretty well hidden until the lead character finds it. You can't just describe the lead character as beaten when the reader can precede you and see a way, or a number of ways in which he isn't beaten at all. If your story reaches what you believe to be the crisis-point, and you sink your lead into the temporary despair which precedes his last and successful effort, you won't make a very good impression on the reader who thinks, "Why, what's wrong with that hero, anyway? He can still do this, or that, or that." And he won't find much to admire when the hero finally wakes up and solves the problem in a way of which the reader had thought minutes before.

You can't, therefore, allow your lead character to be defeated in a number of attempts to solve his problem, and then, arbitrarily, run him through one additional defeat and call that one the last of the possibilities, the crisis-point, when it isn't. That is where your limits come in so handy; you can work up a problem which has a limited number of solution possibilities (plus one which you make sure is chosen carefully enough so that the reader can't easily anticipate it), and then reach your crisis-point when all the possibilities except the one you've saved have been exhausted. Thus you have a satisfactory crisis—because it really looks as though your lead character is sunk—and you still have a good, unpredictable solution possibility on hand to use for the finish.

Your lead character must be at the lowest depth of despair at the crisis-point: even in the stories which go on to end unhappily. In the ultraliterary story previously described, for example, where the story ends with the lead character's decision that You Can't Win, he is at a lower ebb at the crisis because he is most deeply confused and bewildered, and not yet (as he is at the end) more or less comfortably resigned to his fate.

Never force your crisis; it must be the inevitable result of the preceding events in the story. Assure its inevitability by making your basic problem extremely difficult to solve, and by using every event in your story to make it become more difficult. If every event pushes your lead character deeper and deeper into a pit, it is inevitable that he will eventually touch bottom—and that is your crisis-point.

I would like to stress once again—and I can't do it too often—that the lead character's failure at his efforts to solve the problem which move the story toward the crisis-point, must be logical, natural, and "the things which would happen under those circumstances." If you find that the only way you can complicate matters for your lead character is by having him do something illogical or stupid, toss out that complication and think some more until you have one which makes matters worse *despite* the fact that the lead acts intelligently and events occur naturally. Your reader departs the moment your character acts stupidly; he is no longer in sympathy with him. He also departs the moment your character acts illogically or events occur unnaturally (such as a big coincidence or too many little ones); he no longer believes the story at all.

Whenever possible, make the problem so difficult that the solution possibilities are uncertain and off-chance at best, so that the lead character's failures will be logical, and won't reflect unfavorably on him. The story will also, of course, move smoothly and inevitably to the crisis if the solution possibilities are bowled over in rapid succession.

Keep your story at the crisis-point just long enough to convince the reader thoroughly that the lead character is sunk and the problem will not be solved. Then, just as soon as he's convinced, show him he's wrong by sending the lead character zooming up the final stretch to the solution.

14

AND THAT DID THE TRICK: *The solution*

This is a true story which has become one of the industry's favorite anecdotes.

Magazines today won't purchase and print each installment of a serial as the author completes it: they've seen so many good stories fall apart at the end that it is now the rule to see and okay the full yarn before they begin to publish any part of it. Some years ago, however, many magazines made it a regular practice to rush into print each installment of a serial as the author pulled it out of his typewriter, and the editors of one of these publications found themselves rather worried one day.

They'd just published the next-to-last installment of a serial, and the author had left the lead character, whom we shall call Lance O'Neill, in quite a fix. After a long series of narrow escapes from death at the villain's hands, the crisis had arrived —and it looked as though Lance were really cooked this time. He had fallen into a deep pit set up by the villain, a pit with sides so smooth it was obvious he wouldn't possibly be able to scramble up again. Sharp spikes were beginning to come out of the sides of the pit to impale him, and, to make things worse, molten lead was beginning to pour out of a pipe in the pit and fill it up.

The more the editors thought about it, the more it worried them. What if the author couldn't think of a solution—some way to rescue O'Neill? What if he found he just couldn't go on,

and they had to publish the next issue without the final installment? The thought was terrible—thousands of readers might
cancel their subscriptions in protest.

Frantically, they phoned the author at his home, but he wasn't
there. They were running down the list, and phoning places at
which he might be found, when he walked in. "What's all the
excitement about?" he asked.

"The Lance O'Neill serial," the editor-in-chief said nervously.
"The predicament he's in—did it throw you? Were you able to
get him out of it?"

Casually, the author took the manuscript of the final installment out of an envelope, and pointed to the opening line. This
is what it said:

With a mighty leap, Lance O'Neill sprang out of the pit.

Unless you can get an editor in a similar fix—and, as I say, it's
impossible because of the current policy of purchasing only
full stories—you'll have quite a time trying to sell your stuff if
you finish up with solutions of that sort. It is the perfect example
of the big build-up which leads to the big letdown.

It is a little difficult to imagine what the author's motives
may have been in solving his problem in that way. It makes a
wonderful little anecdote, but it is incredibly inexpert plotting
technique. Perhaps the circumstances made the sale so certain
that he just didn't give a damn; perhaps, like the writers of that
movie described in Chapter 12, he had written himself so deeply
into a jam that he could see no other way out. But whatever his
motives, he certainly did not expect his readers to believe that
O'Neill could spring out of a pit, however mighty his leap,
which had been described as too deep and steep to climb.

Aside from giving the publishing field an anecdote to cherish,
Lance O'Neill's mighty leap accomplished only one thing; it
sprinkled vanishing cream over the reading audience and made
it disappear. An audience will always leave a story which it has
ceased to believe; it will depart in an annoyed mood when it

does not believe the solution, because that is the moment for which it has been waiting ever since the story began. To hold your reader by building up and building up and building up a problem, and then have the lead character resolve it through unbelievable, illogical, or downright silly means, is to bunch insult and injury together with one sudden kick to the reader's trousers.

Believability, then, is the first thing for which to watch when you are mapping out your solution. You discard it when you do any of these things:

1. When the lead character solves his problem by doing something which is obviously beyond his powers, as in the O'Neill story. A good story gives an accurate gauge of a character by his activities throughout; you begin to know the things he can do and cannot do, his exceptional qualities, and the qualities he lacks. He must, therefore, resolve his problem by means which are possible, by an act of which he is capable. Certainly he must make a superior effort to do so after the crisis—certainly he must put everything he has into it—but he cannot, without reason, suddenly be capable of doing things he could not do before that.

2. The problem must remain as knotty as ever throughout his solution activities; it must not miraculously be simplified for him. The O'Neill story, looking at the other side of the coin, is off in this way, too: because, if you are to believe that O'Neill could spring out of the pit, then it must not have been as deep as you had supposed it had been pictured. In that case, the basic problem itself is weak—for the pit was the *pièce de résistance,* the culmination and the crowning of all the villain's evil attempts on O'Neill's life. If the villain can't do better than a shallow pit from which a man can jump, he's not so tough that he's worth worrying about too hard.

The same principle and objection applies to all other examples: such as the story in which the inexperienced tenderfoot is forced into a gun battle with a quick-drawin' hombre and, amazingly, outdraws him (only to discover afterward that the quick-drawin' villain had injured himself while scratching the small of his back a few minutes before). The reader will find it difficult to believe that Fate, which has buffeted the lead character around all through the story, will suddenly decide to be so good to him at the crucial moment. The lead may, of course, push the odds on his side through his own efforts: for example, by setting the location of the gun duel so that the blinding sun shines in the villain's eyes and his own vision remains clear.

3. Likewise, any other solution by means of sudden good fortune or accident will be eyed dubiously; the sudden arrival of the rich and check-bestowing uncle from 'Mwbongo, a wealthy suburb in Tanganyika, or the sudden observing of a thick lump in the mattress which turns out to be a cache stashed away and then forgotten by the room's previous occupant (the exact amount, $837.56, which the lead needs).

There is only one way in which unexpected good fortune, or the unexpected appearance of a new talent or ability on the part of the lead character, can be credibly handled: when an earlier clue or plant reveals that the good fortune or talent might have been unexpected by the reader, but not by the lead himself. If, for example, Lance O'Neill had mentioned casually, while leaping over a mud puddle in an early part of the story, that he had won all field events during the last Olympic Games, it would have been more credible when he had leaped out of that pit (stating meanwhile that he had once done three inches better at the standing high jump at college).

The big headache about plants, of course, is that they must be inserted visibly enough so that the reader will say, "Gosh, that's right," when the lead uses his special ability or the good fortune occurs, and it is revealed to have been foreshadowed; and yet not obviously enough so that the reader will spot it and yawn in bleak anticipation when the crisis-point arrives and the lead begins the action toward the solution. The best way to accomplish it is to plant the fact that the lead has the special ability, or has begun to turn the wheels which may bring him the later good fortune, as a part of an earlier effort to solve his problem, so that the reader will not suspect that it will have later significance. It's a touchy business; study lots of plants in published stories before you try one yourself.

4. The too pat solution, where so many things turn out right that it goes beyond the realm of possibility. If your lead character is an escaped con who has broken loose just to murder an old enemy, and in the end understands the error of his ways— due to his love of a girl he's met—and goes back to prison, there is no need for the warden to like him suddenly and turn his back so that the lead can escape again to live happily with the girl, or for the governor to rush forward with a blanket pardon. You see this in new writers' stories all the time: the lead solves his problem, and immediately the entire world seems to sense it, and everybody acts like a sympathetic character out of the Oz stories. The lead has redeemed himself in his own eyes, and will presumably get together with the girl when he finishes his term; but you can bet that he'll have to finish it, and probably a bit more as well, as punishment for the escape. Solve the problem, certainly, but don't break out into a gigantic rash of good fellowship and have everybody else in the story, even the unsympathetic characters, begin to act like Santa Claus.

Plausibility is one important consideration in planning your solution; proper selection is another.

The all-important purpose of the solution is that it must settle the problem in the most logical and most satisfying way possible—it must take the final step which moves the story to its most suitable destination.

As I have explained earlier, this does not mean that the solution must always be the one the lead character most desires; not at all. It must, however, always be the one which is most logical in view of the earlier occurrences in the story, and which most logically settles the problem.

Sometimes the story *must* end unhappily—or with a mixture of sadness and happiness, as in the bittersweet stories which the slicks often use. (Lead loses his child, despite his frenzied efforts to save her during her illness, but the basic problem is solved—his struggles bring him and his wife together though they had begun to drift apart.) Sometimes a story must end indefinitely. (For example, lead breaks up with his wife because he believes he is in love with a younger woman, later returns to his wife. It would be illogical, and unnatural, if she takes him back at once and their life together immediately resumes its normal course. This story must end indefinitely to end logically; the reader *must* be left only with the hope that they'll eventually be the same again.) Sometimes a story will end with the problem completely overcome and eliminated; sometimes, as in some quality stories, it must end with the problem still unbeaten—but settled in the sense that the lead now understands it and is prepared to fight it forever if necessary, or is resigned to it and will try to live happily despite its unremovable presence.

The story which ends with the problem overcome and eliminated is perhaps most easily salable, but any of these types of solutions is good if it is the *right* solution for the story. Don't force an unhappy ending because you've had a bad breakfast and feel morbid that day; or tack on an illogical and contrived happy ending just because you think it is the thing to do. Let the solution stem from the rest of the story; if it is satisfactorily and irrefutably the only solution which could logically come from the problem and the other events in the story, it is *right.*

I've already said a thing or two about the importance of resolution of the problem through the lead character's own efforts; let me say just a little more.

The important thing is that you do not show the lead up as

so weak-charactered that he sits around numbly while someone else solves his problem, or so inept that he fails to solve his problem while someone else comes along and succeeds. He must, as I have said, be worthy of the reader's sympathetic attention.

That means that he must be the motile power in the working out of his own salvation; it does not mean that he has to be Superman. If, in other words, he discovers that he can save himself (and, perhaps, the others in his group) from attacking bandits by rolling a huge boulder down the side of a mountain, it doesn't mean that he must pry the rock loose and heave it downward all by himself; he can get help from the others, but he should be the one to think of the boulder. If he succeeds in locating the gang of twenty killers in a deserted edge of town, he doesn't have to play the comic-magazine hero by attempting to capture them all single-handed, which might make readers scorn his good sense as easily as it might make them admire him. He can call the police, and perhaps later have a private tussle with the chief villain, whom he catches trying to sneak out of a secret exit; the important thing is that he has worked his own salvation by locating and getting the killers captured.

Don't go out of your way to have your lead character act so heroic that he's unbelievable; but don't let him sit around like a brachycephalic while others work for him, either.

Throughout these past few chapters, which discuss the plot skeleton in detail, you've noted, I trust, that there are a great many holes into which your foot can slip. That, I think, answers better than anything else the question of how much prewriting planning is necessary.

The better your plot plan before you begin writing—the more closely you have checked each of the many considerations which come up in the writing business—the better your chances of producing consistently good and salable stories. As far as I'm concerned, such story-planning practices as writing up long life histories of each character are nonsense, because I cannot see where they help in any way; but it *is* a good idea to plan your plots thoroughly and carefully enough so that you don't waste your writing time on junk.

15

WHO TELLS IT?: *Viewpoint*

Back around 1880, one of the most popular methods of story-telling was the omniscient-viewpoint method, also known as the author-intrusion method. Viewpoint in fiction simply means the person through whose eyes and other senses the story action is seen, and the omniscient viewpoint featured the author as a sort of official and visible narrator who described the characters' actions and stepped in and analyzed their emotions or made other comments whenever he felt it necessary. As a result, the reader would get paragraphs like this:

Genevieve looked up into the handsome stranger's glittering black eyes. "Very well, sir," she said. "I'll come up to your apartment tonight to discuss my new job as your secretary." Alas, poor Genevieve! Your heart flutters only in anticipation of your new job, and not because you are aware that you are in danger. Be careful, innocent Genevieve! The handsome stranger is not the impersonal, kindhearted gentleman he seems!

The author would also stop the action on occasion to moralize or make a direct comment to the reader:

Van Stuyvesant lurched drunkenly toward her. Demon Rum, that evil beast which inflames men's minds, had taken hold of his senses. O liquor, that terrible and foul master! Better that you, good reader, may never know its horrors.

The omniscient-viewpoint story still turns up on the unrush piles (and, subsequently, in the rejection baskets) at magazine offices all the time. The old-fashioned language is gone, and the author may not sink into coy vapors at each minor moral misstep, but he is still around to nudge the reader familiarly every once in a while and interpret or comment upon the characters' actions. A paragraph from a modern omniscient story might read something like this:

John walked briskly toward the general manager's office. He'd have been better off if he'd left well enough alone and stayed out of the matter entirely, as he was to find out, but he wasn't quite bright enough to realize it then. He knocked on the door.

There are two important things wrong with the use of the omniscient viewpoint in fiction. The first is that a good story holds the reader because it gives the temporary illusion of reality while he's reading it—because he believes it and gets deep in it during the reading—and the intrusion of the author or the author's comments snaps him out of it each time and reminds him that it is, after all, just a story. Frequently, as in the example given, the author's intrusion describes the shape of things to come, and there's no better way to destroy the illusion of reality than to remind the reader that future events are all mapped out and ready to be brought on-stage.

And the second fault of the omniscient-viewpoint story is that its author-intrusion characteristic does not help the story in any real way, but tends instead to distract. Where the author describes the emotions of the characters, it would be better to show the characters feeling those emotions and thus bring the reader to know and understand them better; where the author comments on the results of their actions, it would be better to let the story show the results. The best place, in short, for the author, is off the set pulling invisible puppet strings, not on the set, directing so much attention to himself that the readers must keep looking away from what the characters are doing.

Shortly after the omniscient-viewpoint story began its decline and fall, the observer-viewpoint story came in for a certain amount of popularity. This is the type in which the story is told by an observer or narrator, who usually takes no part or only a minor part in the story events.

Most of the older observer-viewpoint stories were "frame" stories; that is, the author drew a sort of picture frame around them by including a little introductory scene before the story proper and a little closing scene after it. The usual frame was one in which a number of people sat around talking, hit on a particular topic, and then one of the people told a tale (the story proper) which illustrated the topic of discussion; after which, for a paragraph or two, the manuscript returned to the conversationalists and they made concluding remarks. Most of P. G. Wodehouse's earlier Mulliner and Oldest Member stories are frame stories.

Frame stories have pretty much vanished from the current literary scene because of one obvious fact—since the frame is almost always nothing more than an introduction and a concluding comment to the story proper, the story proper is better off without it. All the frame does is hold up the arrival of the real story, and then hold the reader for an unnecessary moment after the real story is over. The form vanished during the modern trend toward getting the story in motion as early as possible. It will undoubtedly stay away.

And, for exactly the same reason, the nonframe observer story—which hasn't got the elaborate build-up, but still starts with a narrator announcing he's going to tell a yarn about someone else (for example: "I'll never forget the day young Joe Delaney first hit town. . . .")—is objectionable. However short the narrator's opening remarks, even if only one or two lines, they are still unnecessary or in the way—because the story really doesn't start until attention focuses in full on the lead character, the man about whom he's talking. Things would be far better off if the observer were left out entirely, and the story begun at once with the appearance of the lead character. Furthermore, the observer-viewpoint story always keeps the reader from getting to know the lead character quite as well as he might; for the observer, being human, can only describe the lead character's emotions as he assumed them to be from outward appearances "when the events occurred." He cannot, as a directly told story may, look right into the lead character's mind.

The best way to tell your story is directly and entirely from the lead character's viewpoint, so that everything which occurs in the story is seen and heard and emotionally felt and judged by the lead character. Remember that your chief hope in writing your stories is that you'll make your reader identify himself so closely with the lead character that he'll almost join him in fighting his problem and living the events in the story. It is logical, obviously, that you stand the best chance of accomplishing this if your manner of narration of the story occurrences parallels the manner in which life occurs: this is, with the lead character (you or me) always on stage, and knowing of events which occur off stage (away from us) by hearing or being told of them.

Your reader is used to the movement of life in this manner; he can more easily identify himself with the lead character and follow him along when the lead character's life moves in the same way. When, however, the story—which is the life the reader is temporarily living if he is fully identified with the lead character—follows the lead and his emotions only occasionally, and keep switching off to events in which the lead does not appear or is not observing (however pertinent they may be to the lead's problem), the movement becomes unnatural and the tight chain of reader-identification is broken. In real life, there is no switching off of consciousness while things away from the lead character's vision are taking place. Exactly the same thing applies to stories which delve into the lead character's emotions, but delve into all the other characters' emotions as well—that is, which don't just describe the hero's emotions and *indicate* the other characters' emotions by the lead character's observations of their actions and reactions, but which leap nimbly from one character's thoughts to another. Easy identification with the lead character is barred to the reader when he knows all these thoughts because it is obvious that the lead character cannot know them.

When the scene shifts without the lead character shifting along with it, or things are revealed in the story whose knowledge the lead character cannot possibly share, the mechanics are showing—it is obviously a story. And full identification is possible only when the reader is made to forget for a while that he's reading a story, and thinks he's living a life.

Many new writers groan when they are advised that shifting or multiple viewpoints are to be avoided, and yet that advice is as sound as it is valuable. The loudest groan results from the fear that these *must* be used—or what does one do when a scene is needed where the lead character cannot be present? Well, the answer is that you gotta when you gotta; if the story cannot possibly be written without a shift away from the lead character's viewpoint, you have no choice but to shift away. Most of the time, however, some careful, logical juggling in your plotting will put your lead character on stage always—which, as the most important character in your story, is where he should always be anyway.

One other type of viewpoint which is dangerous is the objective viewpoint, as used in some of Ernest Hemingway's stories —where the emotions of the lead character and the others in the story are not described or touched upon at all, and only a straight and objective job of reporting is done. Sometimes, as in the Hemingway stories, the events are so dramatic, and the participants' reactions to them so obvious, that a straight-reporting job will suffice. Most of the time, however, the reader will react emotionally because the character reacts emotionally.

Emotion is part of your writing stock-in-trade: why avoid it?

As you continue to read magazines, you'll run across occasional stories with multiple viewpoints, observer viewpoints, and omniscient viewpoints. Sometimes you'll run across quite a batch at once. The answer is the same one which applies to all writing rules, but let me state it this time in another man's words—those of a prominent editor who recently gave a lecture on the importance of using the lead character's viewpoint throughout the story, and was asked why his own magazine sometimes used shifting- and multiple-viewpoint stories.

"You know," the editor said, "we've got a cook at home who prepares everything wonderfully except potato pancakes—and I like potato pancakes. Despite this, we hired her when she applied, because all the other cooks the agencies had sent over had more faults, and we really needed a cook." He paused. "I often think, though, that she ought to go off in a corner of the kitchen one time and learn how to prepare good potato pancakes. Someday she may have to apply for another job, and that time her competition may be stiffer."

The point, of course, is that sometimes stories are bought despite their faults, but it is safer to avoid the faults if possible.

There are two reasons which make it preferable that you write many more third-person stories than first-person. One is that editors buy far more third-person stories than first-person; the other is that the first-person form is extremely restricting.

You can describe the lead character's physical appearance in third-person stories. You can show his emotional reactions through his physical reactions (for example: *his face grew red with anger; his lips whitened with fear; hate showed in her eyes; his expression was bleak and icy; his lips twisted with bitterness;* and so on). When a first-person lead character describes his physical appearance, however, or describes too often his own physical or emotional reactions, he sounds either unnatural or like a too self-centered ass.

About the only time first-person storytelling is preferable to third is when the fact that the entire story is told in the lead character's own idiom or unusual manner characterizes him more deftly or accurately. You can, for example, build up a character as tough or cocky by his actions and conversation in a third-person story, but sometimes the fact that, in effect, he does *all* the talking in a first-person story will accomplish this more properly. In almost all other cases, the third-person story is preferable.

The other forms—second-person, stories told in the plural— are trick types which editors buy once in an ultramarine moon. Do them as often. Stories told in letter or telegram form belong in the same category, but more so. Editors once considered this an original and clever method of storytelling, but it has been done so often through the years that they'll rarely buy one today except from the men who made the type famous, such as Richard Sherman and William Hazlitt Upson.

16

WHAT MAKES THEM TICK?: *Motivation*

Recently, a man in Seattle walked into a restaurant and ordered a porterhouse steak, rare. When the steak was brought, he called for the proprietor, and complained that the steak was too well done. The proprietor looked at the steak and insisted it was rare. They argued back and forth for a moment, and abruptly the customer concluded the discussion by seizing his meat knife and stabbing the proprietor through the heart.

Recently, a Cincinnati woman left for Reno to file suit to divorce her husband. This action stunned her friends, who had known the couple to be extremely well matched and well adjusted and happy. The woman explained that her husband was a good man and admirable and lovable in almost every way, but he had been entirely too mean to her cat.

Recently, a wealthy and attractive widow in a small town in Illinois chose a husband from among a dozen men who had been courting her. All of them had been nice and she had had a terrible time choosing, so, she told a local reporter quite seriously, she had finally chosen So-and-so because he had such wonderful taste in ties.

These are real-life motivations for murder, divorce, and marriage. All of these incidents actually happened; all were reported as oddities during a television newscast. Try to use them in a story, however, and see how far you get.

They are not necessarily studies in abnormal psychology or

behavior, either. Court records, news magazine files, and everyday gossip are jam-packed full of stories of everyday people, otherwise quite normal and rational, who have done one cockeyed thing in their time. That includes you and me. You and I, undoubtedly, have never murdered anyone in a fit of pique— at least I haven't, and I hope *you* haven't—or undertaken such major steps as marriage or divorce for such minor reasons, but all of us have done a few things in our lives which we'd admit (to ourselves, anyway) are atypical or odd. The cliché experts have an answer for it; they say, shrugging, that people are people.

Well, people may be people and sometimes do funny or irrational things, but your story people cannot because they must be "typical" people. Let me show you what I mean.

When a person in real life does something strange, or without an adequate motive or reason, you may scratch your head over it or wonder about it—but there is no possibility that you will disbelieve it because you know that it *has* happened. A character in a story, however, is in another situation entirely: let him do something incredible or without adequate motivation, and the reader immediately realizes that the whole thing is made up and doesn't believe any of it.

Let us say that your cousin Hortense married her husband mostly because she just loved the way he whistled "Stardust," and so you have your heroine in your story select her mate because she loves his skill at whistling. Your readers, however, do not know Cousin Hortense, and it is extremely unlikely that they know anyone else who chose a husband on the basis of his whistling skill. Therefore, they scoff at this motive because they don't know it to be true, and because it is certainly not a typical motive for mate choice—just as you would not believe many real-life occurrences if you did not know for sure that they actually happened.

You're not just telling a little true occurrence to your friends, relatives, and others who are likely to take you at your word, when you're writing a story—you're turning out something which, if it sells to a magazine, will be read by hundreds of thousands or even millions of people. All kinds of people—farmers and city slickers and office workers and pick-and-shovel laborers—the innocent and the too wise people who'll believe everything, and people who must be convinced before they'll believe *anything*. In order to give your characters adequate and believable motivation for everything they do, therefore, you must give them the most typical and logical motivation—the thing *most* people would do under those circumstances.

That makes the motivation believable at once—why should the character's reason for doing something be incredible when anybody would do what he's doing for the same reason? It is only when the character's motives and actions are different from the normal—when he does something for an inadequate reason, or when he does exactly the opposite of what a normal person in that position might be expected to do—that it is disbelieved. The fact that a few people in real life may have acted that way doesn't alter things; you're not going to be able to hand out a signed affidavit to this effect with each copy of the magazine printed.

There's a technical name for it: the factor of mass reasoning *vs.* individual reasoning. It is another way of saying the same thing—reasons for particular actions are believable when they are what the mass, the majority of people, would do under those circumstances, and they are not necessarily believable because a few scattered individuals may have done things that way.

People generally act in character. If the average weak and cowardly man should walk into a bank and see that it is being held up, he would faint, not leap forward unarmed and attack the *banditti*. On a number of occasions in real life, perhaps, some peculiar chemistry may have caused normally cowardly individuals to reverse themselves under stress and turn into heroes—but an unmotivated character change of this sort will rarely be digestible in fiction.

When you develop a character along specific lines, as you always must—when you show him to be a particular kind of person—his motivations throughout, his reasons for doing whatever he does in the story, must be exactly in line with the way most people of that type would act under those circumstances. If he is built up throughout as a brave hero, and no clue is ever given to the fact that he is really a big bluff and a coward underneath it all, it will be unbelievable if he suddenly, without reason, begins to act cowardly. If you build up a character as a timid person who turns pale every time he has to cross a busy intersection, because he's afraid he might get hurt, you can't suddenly, for no visible reason, have him change to an intrepid person who grins as he turns to face an escaped lion, and, never pausing in his whittling, kicks the lion's hindquarters all the way back to the circus grounds. (The real-life man who changed under stress from cowardice to heroism may have done so, perhaps, because fear brings a double dose of adrenalin. This isn't adequate reason for the change in fiction, however; adrenalin can also help a coward run away twice as fast.) Your motivation, in short, will be sound only if the character always acts typically—always acts like the kind of person you have shown him to be.

This does not mean that your characters need ever be stock types, made out of familiar molds; and it doesn't mean that the events in the story need ever be routine. If you really understand the people in your story and are completely positive about the way they would act and react under various circumstances, you may make them as unusual, or their adventures as unusual, as you wish. All that is important is that they remain consistent throughout. The reader will certainly know it if they don't, even though he may never have run across circumstances *exactly* like those in real life.

If, for example, you want to write a story which ends with

a scene in which the hero turns on an escaped lion and pushes him back in his cage, you may certainly go ahead and do so: provided you have built up your hero as a fearless fellow who has grown up among lions (his father was a zoo keeper) and he knows just how to handle them. The point again is consistency of action, typical action; a brave man with that background might well do what the hero does. It would only look ridiculous if the intersection-fearing character acted that way when confronted by a lion; but it doesn't look ridiculous when, let us say, Tarzan acts that way in pictures, because Tarzan has been built up believably as a man who does everything but yawn when kings of the jungle menace him. The reader doesn't have to have lion-fighting friends to understand and believe this, or to regard the timid man's lion-shooing as out of character and the courageous zoo keeper's son's shooing as believable. If he's ever seen a circus, he knows there are people who can handle them; on the other side of the coin, he's surely met cowards. Maybe he's even a coward himself; heck, *photos* of lions scare *me*.

Nor does consistency in motivation mean that stories which include drastic character changes must be unbelievable. On the contrary, of course, there have been hundreds of thoroughly logical and believable stories written along those lines. The important thing is that the change must come for strong, well-motivated reasons.

It may come, for example, if the heroine turns bitterly away from the timid lead character, disgusted at his cowardice, and he is *forced* to be heroic because he'll lose her forever if he isn't—as a result of which he discovers that it isn't so hard being a brave man, after all. Or, let us say, the tough, deadly, close-mouthed villain has one chink in his armor—a pathological fear of rats, established early in the story—and the hero breaks his spirit and makes him shaken and open-mouthed by locking him overnight in a vermin-ridden cell.

When you do this sort of thing in your story, you aren't causing your story people to act out of character—you're merely causing them to act in a new way which is right because they've undergone a perfectly logical and reasonable *change* in character. What you have done, in effect, is to put two strong facets of their character at war, and allowed the stronger facet to win. Fear is strong in the timid hero, but his love for the heroine is stronger, and so his character changes—and he by-passes his former mode of action (cowardice) and acts bravely, as his new character demands. Toughness is strong in the villain, but his pathological fear of rats is strong too—and it becomes the stronger of the two and overpowers the other when the hero magnifies it by forcing the villain to remain overnight in the vermin-filled cell.

If you really understand people as you should, you're familiar with the basic drives which make them act as they do—love, hate, fear, greed, jealousy, the struggle for security, and so on. Use them to motivate your characters, or to cause character change. And make sure, most of all, that you never make your characters act illogically, or do things without adequate reason, just because you want to keep the story rolling.

17

BUT WHO'LL BELIEVE IT?: *Plausibility*

The means of assuring plausibility in your stories is an extension or enlargement of the method by which you assure logical and adequate motivation. It is, in other words, the same principle of mass or majority *vs.* individual, applied to everything in your story rather than just to the characters' reasons for doing what they do.

In gauging the logic or adequacy of your characters' motivations, you use the yardstick of whether or not most real-life people would act or react in that way under those circumstances. In gauging the plausibility of things other than motivation in your stories, you use the yardstick of whether or not events most usually happen that way, or would most logically happen that way.

Coincidence, for example, is implausible because it is not the way things most usually happen—because, in short, it is the way things may have happened in comparatively rare *individual* real-life cases, but not the way things happen in the *mass* or *majority* of real-life cases. Most people who are in trouble in real life don't get out of it through the receipt of an unexpected big check, or through the fortuitous discovery of a large sum of money in an old mattress at the exact moment of most extreme need. Most people who are in trouble in real life just don't have the good luck of seeing the one-person-who-can-help-them turn up out of the distant past at the crucial moment. (*"Good gad, prisoner—I'd know that diamond-shaped birthmark on your neck anywhere! Aren't you the son of old Yancey Doodle, who used to be a horse ostler in Memphis? He once gave me two crusts of bread and a dab of peanut butter when I was a starving young lawyer—before I became the famous, well-respected, lovable, and distinguished judge I am now. Son, the charges of murder, blackmail, kidnaping, arson, conspiracy to overthrow the government, armed robbery, counterfeiting, forgery, and expectoration in the subway are dismissed!"*)

Things of that sort, much modified, *have* happened—the arrival of coincidental good luck at times when it is most needed —but these occurrences are so few and far between that each one usually rates considerable publicity as an oddity. Most of the time, people in real life get out of their troubles through plenty of toil and struggle, and that is the way it must be in fiction.

By the same token, as explained earlier, coincidental *bad* luck is just as implausible—where the complications do not occur as unfortunate but natural results of the hero's efforts to solve his problem, but where they happen without build-up or reason just so things can be tougher for the hero. If the hero, for example, is on his way somewhere to solve his problem, and just happens to trip on a loose rock and breaks his leg, the story becomes "contrived"—that is to say, the author is *making* things happen, instead of letting things happen as natural results, as in real life. If, on the other hand, the hero is forced, in order to solve his problem, to climb a shaky structure which he knows may break down and injure him, and it does and he breaks his leg, there's nothing contrived or implausible about it—it's a natural result.

Few people in real life actually receive what might be called the "Job treatment" by Fate—more and more bad luck just happening to pile up on an original piece of bad luck or trouble. Even those pyramids of minor troubles—those days where everything seems to go wrong—are less often series of coincidences in real life than they are "the unfortunate but natural results of the lead character's efforts to solve his problem." Your basic problem arrives (the alarm clock fails to go off and you may be late for work) and thereafter almost everything else which goes wrong—the burning of the toast, the spoiling of the eggs, the putting on of the wrong suit, etc.—stems from the fact that you're rushing so much to solve your problem and get to work on time that you flub the other things. And by then, of course, you've put yourself in such a nervous state that you flub everything else through the day, and magnify the other few annoyances which just happen, when, ordinarily, you'd ignore them.

Dig into your own experience, and you'll find that the cases of serious bad luck piled on serious bad luck in real life are so rare that they have become local legends. They certainly aren't sufficiently in the majority, or typical enough, to be plausible in fiction.

Coincidences don't have to be king-size to do injury to your story, either; even little things which just happen to happen can be harmful. The safe just happens to have been left open by mistake the day the hero sneaks into the house to search for the missing papers—the heroine gets lost and just happens to stop for directions at the farmhouse where the villain is hiding out—any event which "just happens" and is too convenient to the story is suspect. When you're about to sling in a too convenient event on the grounds that, well, it's *possible,* remember that the test of plausibility in fiction is whether or not it's *probable.*

Usually, triteness in a story brings with it a strong odor of implausibility. Coincidence and contrived complications fail to satisfy readers because they seem too obviously invented, or made up because they lack the necessary aura of reality or real life. In the same way, many trite situations and character types are grinned at today because they've been used so often in stories and have become so heavily identified with fiction that readers can no longer square them up with actuality or real life.

There are, I suppose, still some hardhearted bankers and property owners who heave out tenants if they are fifty-five seconds beyond the final deadlines allowed for their mortgage or rental payments, and still a goodly number of young ladies who are told that they may make mortgage or rental payments through the temporary or permanent loan of what is euphemistically known as their honor. There are, according to police records, even a number of cases where people have been murdered or forced to yield up secrets by being tied to railroad tracks while the train loomed not too far in the distance. Just try to use these little items in stories today and sell them, however—I dare you.

The death of many of these trite items, of course, has been helped along by the fact that people have become, with the spread of communication and entertainment facilities, far more sophisticated in their fiction tastes and their hunt for realism. They know now that many of the mellerdrammar situations and character types (in which they once believed so faithfully) never existed at all, or at least not as generally as they had supposed. Certainly even during the financial panics of the eighteen-seventies and eighteen-eighties, when a great many people did find themselves homeless, the amount of hard-hearted eviction specialists in fiction was out of all proportion to those in real life, so you might call it the factor of mass *vs.* individual at work again. Some trite items, too, have been given the final push into their graves by changes in custom which altered them from everyday occurrences to rarities; for example, the implausibility today—due to the decrease of parental control over children—of the once quite logical parental-objection complication in romantic stories.

The absent-minded professor was a quite acceptable character in the less critical era; today this fellow who reacts to rainstorms by putting his open umbrella on his head and holding his hat up in the air is generally considered implausible because people measure him against their own teachers and know that extremely few, if any, are that sort of muddleheaded nincompoop. You'll also note a steadily decreasing number of comic habitual drunks in fiction, because, aside from the consideration of taboos against drunkenness, today's knowledgeable reader realizes that most habitual drunks are frightening or pitiful rather than funny. The same thing applies to yesterday's too positive, too black-or-white types—the Hairbreadth Harry hero who does everything out of innate goodness and the villain who does everything out of innate evil. It is certainly easier to paint a character as all boy scout or all villain and perhaps there *are* a few people on earth who live only to do good or evil for sound personal reasons.

The telltale personal characteristics have gone down the triteness and implausibility drains, too. Readers are no longer naïve enough to believe that a man whose eyes are shifty, or who can't look straight at you during a conversation, is necessarily a crook. It may be nothing more than shyness, while the clear-eyed, fresh-faced chap may pick your pocket while you're busy admiring his clear eyes and fresh face. And it is hardly necessary, I suppose, to tell you that a mustache is no longer a trademark of villainy, particularly if you happen to wear a mustache yourself.

Accuracy of facts is another important factor in the job of assuring plausibility in your stories. There was a time when a little technical mumbo jumbo which *sounded* right would suffice, but not any more. People are better educated today because there are more schools and more rigid attendance requirements; mass magazine, book, and paperback book publishing have spread the reading habit; and the various other entertainment media teach them things, too. Make one factual misstep today, and hundreds of people will write nasty letters. They'll have learned the correct facts of the matter at school, in other books or stories, or in the movies, stage plays, or television.

Many magazines today employ large staffs of experts, or keep experts on call, to check facts in stories before they publish them. A few magazines send writers long lists of questions after they purchase stories. (Here are typical questions: *You describe your character, Arnicho, as a Pole; is the name definitely Polish, or is it Czech, Russian, etc.? Statement on page 4 that men's shoe size 8½ is size most often sold; is this guess, or have you checked it?* You can see that the magazines are quite careful.)

It's bad when an editor catches you off on a fact, and it is downright terrible when he misses it and the readers point it out. He may decide, consciously or subconsciously, that it is dangerous to purchase any more stories from a writer as careless as you. As far as the readers are concerned, it may destroy the plausibility of the entire story for them, particularly if it indicates that you don't know the general subject or background about which you're writing, or if the erroneous fact (or incorrectly described gadget) is the means of bringing about the problem, complications, or solution. I'll have a little more to say about accuracy of facts in the chapter on locale.

An individual or atypical occurrence will never be plausible in a story when you attempt to fob it off on the reader as the typical or natural things which would happen under those circumstances. You may, however, use an individual occurrence if a definite point is made of its individuality, or if that is the entire point of the story.

Let us say that you have learned somewhere that a few dogs have been taught to climb trees. Most dogs, of course, cannot, so a story occurrence would strike the reader as absolutely implausible if a dog had been chasing a cat, and proceeded to chase it right up the trunk of a tree. If, however, the character who owns the dog mentions specifically that Rover can climb trees—and does so in such a way (perhaps by naming actual dogs who have climbed trees and received some fame for it) that the reader realizes some dogs *can*—it will not be implausible if an important development later hinges on the dog's upward climb through the branches.

Fantasy stories are built on the same principle, except that the individual fact is not actually true. The reader gives the author the benefit of one assumption—that, let us say, there *are* werewolves, or space travel to Venus *is* an everyday affair—and the author goes on from there. All the other facts in the story (excepting those concerning werewolves, or travel to or life on Venus, where the author has a free hand) must operate on normal standards of plausibility. The humans must still act like humans, and do things for the reasons most humans do them; all natural events must still happen naturally and logically.

If, then, you decide to do a story about a dog which climbs trees, or a scene in which a man knifes a restaurateur because he believes his steak is too well done, you need not necessarily turn out an implausible job—provided definite backing-up and attention is given to the unusualness of the dog's ability and the steak eater's action. You'll go awry only when you ring in that sort of thing without special heralding, in the blind hope that your readers will be dull witted enough to assume that that is the way those things usually happen.

18

HIS THOUGHTS RETURNED TO HIS CHILDHOOD:
Flashback

A friend of mine named John Hartford once had the harrowing experience of finding himself alone with a homicidal maniac in a self-service elevator stuck between floors. Hartford had noticed another man get into the elevator with him as he hurried into his apartment building, but hadn't thought much about it until the creaky old elevator quit abruptly, as it occasionally did, and stuck between floors. Suddenly the other man began to mutter hoarsely that my friend was a secret agent and had stopped the elevator as a murder trap, and Hartford looked up into the wildest eyes and most horrible face he had ever seen in his life. As he watched, the man said, "I'll kill *you* first," and drew a long, thin knife from his pocket.

Hartford's horror grew when he saw that the blade was already bloodstained.

The man began to move slowly toward him, and, strangely, something about which Hartford hadn't thought for many years flashed into his mind—his last day in Indiana before he had left to live in New York. He thought about the turmoil within him that day, the struggle between his love for his home town and his desire to make good in the big city, and how he might not now be facing death at a madman's hands if he had decided to stay at home. He remembered his Aunt Marian, pleading. "John," she had said that day, "your father tells me you've definitely made up your mind to go to New York. You mustn't do it, John. I've been in New York many times, and . . ."

Tell me, are you anxious to shut Aunt Marian up? Are you chafing at the bit, and anxious to go on finding out what happened to Hartford in the self-service elevator that night? If so, I've succeeded in illustrating the chief reason for general editorial objection to the flashback: its stop-the-story aspect.

The human mind acts strangely when its owner is frightened, and so many thoughts of the past crowded into Hartford's consciousness in those few seconds—the things his Aunt Marian had said, the things his father and mother had said, the things his Uncle Henry had said, the things he had said, even some of the details of his train trip East—that I could go on telling you about them for the next three or four pages. I won't, however, because I know you're interested in the main story line rather than its sidetracks; I almost knifed Hartford myself when he paused in telling his experience to describe in minute detail his fevered reminiscences as the killer approached. Anyhow, to get back to it, Hartford is a pretty fair boxer so, as the lunatic got close to him, he snapped out of his dream and belted the lunatic a couple of times. These put the madman to sleep long enough to enable Hartford to crawl out of the elevator, escape and summon the police.

As in this little true story, flashback has earned its bad reputation because, too often, it interrupts the exciting here-and-now events to fill in background or tell some incident in past history which is neither absolutely relative nor anywhere nearly as exciting. The reader, naturally, doesn't like this, because he has become interested in the here-and-now events—the things which are happening at present in the story—and he wants to go on seeing how things in the here-and-now turn out. As far as he's concerned, therefore, the flashback is merely an annoying interruption, and he may either skip it entirely or skim through it rapidly and apathetically so that he can get back to the interesting things that are happening now.

Let's take an example. Let's take a marriage-problem story in which the heroine and her husband have had a lot of little arguments; but she has always shrugged these off as unimportant and normal until he tells her bluntly one day that he is sick of their constant bickering and has begun to see another woman. After he leaves, she stands there numbly, wondering what she is going to do. She still loves him very much, but she cannot bring herself to try to win him back in view of this certain proof that he no longer loves her.

All right, the reader's on board. He likes the heroine, and he likes her husband, and he thinks they're both a little at fault, and he'd like to see them get together again. It doesn't look as though it will be easy, and his attention is held as he watches the heroine begin to struggle with her problem. But what do you know? Unhappily, the writer has the flashback germ.

So the heroine stands there numbly for a moment, and then a flashback begins. Her thoughts wander, and she begins to remember happier days—when she first met her husband—the courtship. . . .

Perhaps the way in which they met was very amusing. They had both gone into a bookshop to buy a popular new novel, and she got there first and picked up the only copy left, and he wanted it and was rather angry. And then, after a while, they began to talk . . . and had lunch together, and that night he apologized for his boorishness by sending her a complete set of the author's works. Since then, through the years, he has always brought home two copies of each new book by that author, and they always laugh about it.

Nice stuff. Maybe even, if the writer is skillful, heart-warming stuff. But honestly; what has it got to do with the problem?

Little touches of this sort are fine; they help point up the urgency of the problem by underlining the fact that their love was once a beautiful thing and it would be a great pity for it to break up now. But many writers don't confine themselves to little touches; they break out in full-blown flashback, and give the reader a long, drawn-out, detail-by-detail history of the past. The result is that the reader is only annoyed by it, or his interest lessened by it, because it takes him away too long from seeing what is happening to the interesting and urgent problem right now.

Or take another example: the story of a young rancher who discovers that his cattle are being rustled. His thoughts slide back to the past, and the following scenes detail his hardships while pioneering through the West and slowly building up his herds of cattle. Again that sort of thing has some point, because the importance of the problem is underlined by the fact that he had so hard a time getting his ranch and the cattle in the first place. This long, detailed flashback misses its purpose too, however, because it takes so long to give added proof of the *urgency* of the problem that it keeps the reader away too long from his main interest: the story of what is being done to *solve* the problem. It is, in a way, like talking so much to convince a friend that you must borrow his car to get somewhere by three o'clock that you finish your summing-up at four.

So many writers misuse flashbacks and turn them into boring dead-stops-in-the-story-movement that editors have become wary of flashbacks in any shape or form. One to two even state morosely that they think writers are better off if they never use flashback at all.

Actually, of course, that just isn't possible, as even the most morose editors will admit when they are discussing writers who use flashback properly. There are a number of instances where flashback, properly used, is a good thing and vitally necessary.

One of these is the build-up-the-urgency use, as discussed, when done properly. Another is when past events are needed to explain current action; why the hero has come to this particular town to solve his problem, or why the hero is in jail when the story opens with a breaking-out scene. And a third is when an important past occurrence has a definite effect on here-and-now action; when, for example, the hero approaches a fist fight with the villain with great fear because he has a psychological horror of boxing—the result of a boxing accident in childhood which resulted in the death of his friend.

When it is at all possible, try to start your story at the beginning (approximately around the time of the arrival of the basic problem) and follow events chronologically through to the ending (the solution of the problem). That is the simplest way to keep your story line direct, and avoid boring, action-stopping explanations of the past. Sometimes, as I have said, it isn't possible. In some stories where a past event has a definite effect on current events, it would be foolish to start all the way back at scenes of childhood and work up to the adult scenes where the problem first begins. In some stories, where the lead comes to a strange town and meets his problem, the events which bring him to the town are not as important or interesting as the event in the town itself which starts the problem, and it is better to explain the reasons for his trip later—rather than start in his home town and include a lot of unnecessary stuff before he gets to the new place and the problem begins.

In those cases and others like them, of course, flashbacks are necessary, and then the importance focuses on the manner in which flashbacks are handled.

The best way is the flashback which doesn't look like a flashback. It is, in other words, the method in which important facts of the past are doled out to the reader a little at a time, and carefully integrated with present action. This is the kind of flashback you should use most of the time, and it will serve all purposes—whatever your reasons for the flashback may be.

Let's take, by way of example, a Western story by an experienced professional which we sold to a magazine, and then to a television show, a while back. The hero is a blind man who arrives in a strange town and is immediately met by trouble from people who want to keep him out.

The story opened at that point because it was the beginning of his basic problem, but there were two earlier events which had to be covered for clarity of the story and present action. One was the hero's reason for coming to the town; the other was the manner in which he had become blind. The author covered the first of these in a hidden flashback integrated in the scene in which the hero and the heroine first get together in the town:

Then he stopped. The light footsteps he had heard leaving the schoolhouse were running toward him. And when he heard a girl's voice say, "Bill! Bill Andrews!"—the same voice, grown up now, but with the same quality of sweetness—he knew it was Lorna Stone.

He turned and said, "Been a long time, hasn't it?"

She was in his arms and her lips touched his before she answered. "Almost eight years," she said. "Eight years—yet you came right away."

"Us blind fellows ain't kept too busy, Lorna," he said softly.

The here-and-now action in this sequence has not stopped for a split second, yet the author has included all the salient facts of a past occurrence, or several. The reader has watched an active scene which is important to the story, yet he now knows (a) the hero knew Lorna Stone years ago, (b) presumably when they were children, or at least when she was a child, and (c) he has come as the result of her summons. In a later conversation, there is a completely natural mention of her letter, so the reader knows that this is the form her summons took.

The author establishes the facts of the time the hero became blind in a here-and-now fast action scene:

The shot came just when he knew it would—the moment he stepped away from the darkened schoolhouse into the area which pressure on his eyes told him was lighted. For a moment, he felt wild, muscle-stiffening fear, the way he had felt as a kid when owl-hoots killed his mother and dad and fired the bullet which left him alive but blind; and then it passed away. He fell onto his stomach, and his gun leaped forward in his hand.

The childhood occurrence is important to the story because it helps explain his absolute hatred for outlaws, and so the author covers it. By integrating it into the present on-stage action of the story, however, he's done it painlessly, and eliminated the necessity of pausing for story-stopping long looks back.

In the same way, flashbacks which don't look like flashbacks can cover the need for comments on the past in any kind of story. The marriage-problem story, for example, might do it this way:

She walked dully down the street, and stopped in front of Neil's Bookshop to wait for her bus. The sight of the store increased the heavy, sick pain within her. It was there that they had first met—there that a silly little quarrel over the one remaining copy of a book by their favorite author had ended in lunch together "to talk it over." That night Jim had apologized for his part in the quarrel by sending her a complete set of books by the author. Tears stung her eyes, and she turned away and saw that her bus was coming.

Here again the majority of the salient facts of the past event are interspersed with the action, so that no actual stop of the present story and trip to the past has been made. The remaining fact—that Jim now buys two copies of each book, and they laugh about it—can be introduced later in much the same way.

One caution in using flashbacks in this way: don't force them. Don't have your characters think in a peculiar way, or act peculiarly, just so you can ring in the necessary past facts. This sort of thing will never do:

She looked out of the window and saw a boy passing. The boy was wearing a sweater. Sweaters are usually knitted, and that reminded her of knitting, and she remembered with a sob that she had first met Joe at a bar, which was two doors down from a knitting store, or was it a pet shop?

As in everything else in fiction, keep it logical. Work at it and you'll find that you always can.

The integrated, bit-by-bit flashback, as described, can be used in almost all cases. Probably the only exception is where the past event is so important to the story, and so dramatic in itself, that you are positive your story will be improved rather than injured if you use a full-size, visible flashback.

In that case, of course, go ahead and use the full-size flashback. Take the curse off it, however, by making sure of two things. First, make it as interesting as you possibly can, so that the reader won't resent as much the pull away from the here-and-now. And second, try to make it seem as little like a flashback as possible by getting rid of the past tenses promptly.

It is not necessary to load your flashback scenes with those reminders that things *have* happened, rather than *are* happening: the "hads" and the "had hads." The following continues to remind the reader that it's just the past being hashed over:

She had gone to the study to rest for a few minutes, and had fallen asleep. Dan's soft voice had awakened her suddenly.

"Kathie," he had said, "wake up—wake up, please."

She had opened her eyes to see him glaring at her. "What is it, Dan?" she'd asked.

"Your father is back, Kathie," he had told her.

Eliminate the "hads" as quickly as possible, and the scene becomes both easier to read and less a constant reminder that it's past stuff.

She had gone to the study to rest for a few minutes, and had fallen asleep. Dan's soft voice woke her suddenly.

"Kathie," he said, "wake up—wake up, please."

She opened her eyes to see him glaring at her. "What is it, Dan?" she asked.

"Your father is back, Kathie," he told her.

One other type of flashback is the "everything remembered" variety. This is the one in which, let us say, a woman sits in a chair beside the body of her husband, whom she has just killed, and remembers past incidents in their lives (which take up the bulk of the story).

In a sense, this is not as much a flashback story as it is a frame story. In most of these, more than 90 per cent of the story takes place during the remembered events. The opening, the occasional brief returns to the present, and the ending usually serve as nothing more than an introduction, intermediate comments, and concluding comments to the remembered events.

There are two things wrong with the everything-remembered story. The first is that it forces the reader to realize throughout that everything has already taken place before the present, and has already reached a conclusion, which gives him that subconscious feeling of lack of urgency which comes whenever he realizes that, as I've said before, all the action is already worked out and just waiting to be brought on stage. (It would take a psychologist to figure out why, but, no matter what the era in which a story is set, it still generates urgency if the story is told as here-and-now and just-happening—even if the era is One Million B.C. The reader, so to speak, lives in that era while the story is going on. Tell him, however, that this event or that took place before the current time of the story, and he feels that that event has "already happened," so why worry about it?)

And the second is that the sense of urgency is reduced still further because the opening scene "in the present" usually tells how the whole thing is going to turn out. The reader, therefore, is never in the real state of suspense which comes with growing worry over how things are going to finish.

There is only one time when the everything-remembered device is best; when most of the opening events of a story are rather mild, but build up to a powerful conclusion, and the telling of the conclusion or near conclusion *first* serves to grip the reader. It's always best when you can make it the near conclusion, of course, so some suspense on how it's going to end will remain.

All in all, you'd do well to use this type sparingly; it isn't too popular, for the reasons given, with the editors.

19

STRANGE SOUNDS AND SMELLS: *Locale*

I have mentioned several times that anything which halts the steady forward movement of your story, even for a little while, is not so good. This also applies, and very much so, to locale and background.

It used to be quite acceptable practice for the author to stop the story action entirely when he felt that some background painting was required, and proceed to sketch in the surroundings and scenery with thick, unrelieved strokes. A few professionals still do it that way. It has never been entirely satisfactory, however, because it is the natural tendency of most readers to shy away from heavy sections of continuous description, and skim them or skip them entirely. You've probably done it yourself on many occasions: the action stops suddenly and you're confronted by long paragraphs of description, and you flip the page and resume reading where the story movement starts up again.

Descriptions of background and locale are important to the success of your story. They help build and shape the mood— the happy tone in a story is always increased when the surroundings seem just as bright and pleasant as the occurrences, and grimness or horror are always emphasized when the events occur in ugly weather and foreboding surroundings—and they help the reader picture the story events by showing him what things look like as well as what is happening. It is a great pity, therefore, when these purposes are defeated because the descriptions are stuck together in such a boring-looking lump that the reader skips it, and most writers today avoid this danger by employing the same principle as that used in the flashback which doesn't look like a flashback. They break up their descriptions of locale and background into small and palatable doses, and integrate them into the action.

Under the one-blob-of-description method, for example, a house might be described in this way:

Frank paused and looked at the house.

It was a big house, but old, with the look of death and decay about it. It was obvious that it had been standing there for many hundreds of years, and the paint which had once been white was now yellowish and peeling. Here and there, large strips of paint had peeled off completely, revealing the rough wood underneath. Shutters hung loosely from the windows, and one or two seemed ready to fall. The wood of the stairs leading up to the front door was rotten, and the knocker on the front door was rusty and dirty. All in all, it was quite an ugly place.

This description gives the picture, all right, but it stops the story to do it. The integrated method might handle the same effect this way:

Frank walked up the stairs, stepping carefully because the wood underneath his feet looked rotten and as though it might cave in at any moment. The whole place looked that way—paint yellowish and peeling, window shutters hanging loosely and ready to fall, a general look of death and decay. It was, he thought sourly, a hell of a house for an intelligent man like John Drexel to buy.

He used the knocker, and his hand came away covered with rust and filth. When the door opened, a sickening odor of dankness filled his nostrils.

He said, "I want to see Drexel."

Actually, the descriptive phrases need not be packed as closely together in the integrated-with-action method; I've done so here only because I want to keep these examples brief. Frank's reactions to the house may continue, piece by piece, all through his visit there, all through his talk with Drexel.

The one-blob use of description is like seeing scenery in a landscape painting; the other is like seeing it in a motion picture film. In the first, you must make a deliberate stop to see the scenery; in the second, the scenery is introduced unobtrusively into your mind while your attention is held by the action. Since the reader's purpose in staying with the story is to watch the action and see how things come out, you can see why he'll prefer the no-stop method.

In these two examples, I've tried, in addition to the discussion of the advantages of integrated description over dead-stop description, to illustrate another important consideration in this matter of locale. To increase the vividness of the reader's picture of the setting, bring all of the senses into play whenever possible.

The reader, remember, shares vicariously all of the lead character's experiences, and along with them all of his reactions, feelings, and sensations. When the lead notes something with only one sense, so, of course, will the reader.

In the first example, Frank's impressions of the house are entirely visual. He sees the house and notes many things about it, and the picture thus conveyed to the reader is moderately vivid.

The pictures conveyed to the reader by Frank's impressions in the second example, however, are far more vivid because several of Frank's senses have been put to use. His reactions to the place this time are composed of equal parts of the way he *sees* the place (the yellowish and peeling paint, the hanging shutters, etc.), the way he *feels* the place through his sense of touch (the feeling of the treacherous stairs swaying underneath his feet, the feeling of rust and filth on his hand), and the way he *smells* the place (the dank odor in his nostrils).

Observation through one sense is often quite vivid: for example, if you see, through the closed window in your room, a youngster hit by a speeding automobile. The vividness is magnified a thousand times, however, if you are on the spot and also hear the thud and the boy's screams, feel blood splash on you, and smell the odor of screeching tires. Scenes in silent motion pictures were sometimes vivid, but there is no comparison to the vivid effects achieved through the addition of sound. As a reverse example (sound without vision and then the two together) some people still enjoy dramas on the radio, but most people no longer can, since the arrival of television, because they've become used to *two*-sense home entertainment. The one-sense radio drama seems flat and lacking because they receive only 50 per cent of the reactions which come with hearing *and* seeing a television drama.

The use of as many senses as possible in your stories, of course, can be overdone; don't have your lead go around stroking everything in sight and sniffing the air like a retired fire-station hound as the engine goes by. When, however, a description comes up in which more than just the visual sense can logically and normally be employed, you'll increase the vividness by employing the others as well.

Remember, too, that the reader must know what the devil the lead character or the author is talking about if he is going to share the sense reactions. Some foreign locale stories, for instance, have the lead character's nose twitching happily as he sits by the campfire and smells the cooking *'gwobnoogo*. The readers find that sort of reaction mighty hard to share when they don't know what *'gwobnoogo* happens to be, or what it smells like. Is it fish—meat of some kind—vegetables— or tree bark? Your lead character should translate, and, if the object is peculiar to that locale, compare it to something with which the reader will be familiar. (Example: *That night I sat at the campfire, my nostrils twitching hungrily as the odor of cooking 'gwobnoogo, an African bird which tastes just like turkey, was wafted toward me.*)

Foreign phrases which will be familiar and understandable to the average reader need not be explained. The average person knows what *parlez-vous français?* means, and is aware that *Schweinhund* is not an expression of endearment. Unfamiliar words and phrases, however, should be explained to be understood, either by direct translation or by use in a sentence where the context makes it clear. (Example of direct translation: *He approached the peasant.* "Magli wah gagli," *he said.* "Let's you and me fight." The English sentence, of course, is a translation of the foreign sentence. This double standard, a foreign sentence always followed by an English sentence, can make tiresome reading after a while, and it is wise to use explanation by context as often as possible. *"Glunkel!"* *the chieftain said. Rogers smiled.* "Thank you for calling me your friend," *he replied, and they shook hands solemnly.* Or: *The guard rushed into the room, swinging a sharp-bladed* kris. *One swing lopped off Professor Carlisle's head.* You don't need a translator to know that a *kris* is a variety of sword.)

And even in the English language, make sure that your descriptive comparisons are comprehensible to the average reader. It just isn't good sense to show off the fact that you once took a course in advanced bird watching by comparing something to the shape of a gitchee-bird when seen at twilight, or any other such obscure thing. When something smells like honey, say that it smells like honey, and not like the Persian dittle flower (of which three exist on earth, and which also smells like honey). Your reader won't rush to pick up his encyclopedia and find out what you're talking about; he'll just examine the description uncomprehendingly and pass over it, so you'll miss giving him the vivid and clear picture he must get.

It is not necessary to establish an absolute and definite locale in every story you write. If a story can take place in any
town just as easily as in any other, it is not a requirement or
particularly essential that you give the locale a name.

If, however, there will be something in the story which *will*
identify the locale as a particular one—a specific city such
as New York (for example, if a scene takes place in the Empire
State Building observatory), or a specific kind of town such as
a small town (for example, if some aspect of the plot deals
with local farms), or a specific area such as the West Coast or
Florida (for example, if it is essential to the plot that the
heroine take a sunbath in December)—be sure to establish
the fact early in the story that it takes place in that particular
town, kind of town, or area. Don't just leave it vague and un-
stated and then spring it on the reader all at once in the middle
of the story.

Unless you name the specific locale or kind of locale almost
at the beginning of the story, and name any other pertinent
and related aspects such as the weather, the reader's natural
tendency will be to identify the locale and conditions—while
he's identifying the lead character with himself—with his own
locale and conditions. If, therefore, he lives in a small town
and has read the first six pages (in which no locale is named
and the action gives no clue) as having taken place in a small
town, it will come as a shock and a pause in the reality if your
hero suddenly asks the heroine on page 10 to have lunch with
him that night at the Brown Derby. If, in the same way, the sun
is shining outside his window as he reads your story, and he
automatically and subconsciously assumes that the weather is
sunny in the story, it will come as a shock and a disturbance
if you suddenly remember to mention on page 7 that all the
events have been taking place in the pouring rain. The reader
will have to adjust his mind back to the beginning, and revisu-
alize all that has gone before as happening in the slightly more
frenzied atmosphere of a downpour, and that will pull him

out of his semihypnotic state of living along with the lead character.

When you choose a specific locale, make sure that you know it well. That does not mean, as I have said, that it *must* be your own locale or a locale with which you are personally familiar. If you know your locale well enough through study of your encyclopedia, research, discussions with people who have lived in the locale, or the reading of a great many stories about the locale, it will often suffice. You'd better, however, check all specific statements of fact about the locale, and make sure your story people act like the real people—regional idioms, local customs, etc.—in that locale.

But if you don't hate your own locale so much that you can't stand to write about it, why *not* stick to it? Certainly you'll always be safer and more sure-footed that way.

I've already stressed the importance of accuracy in your fiction, and obviously accuracy in matters of locale stands high on the list. You've undoubtedly heard a few examples on the other side of the coin: the most famous being the fact that early editions of Edgar Rice Burroughs' *Tarzan of the Apes* included tigers among the denizens of the African jungle, and the book did wonderfully well, anyhow. Remember that those examples are famous because they're such rare occurrences: they certainly aren't an excuse for carelessness in your own work.

THREE: THE WRITING FACTS

20

LOOKING FOR THE BULL'S-EYE: *Slanting*

You'll hear a great many things about slanting as you amble through this writing business. You'll hear, among other things, that it is a good thing to do, and that it is a bad thing to do, and that it is an easy thing to do, and that it is a hard thing to do.

Well, it is and it isn't. It's a good thing to do if you do it right, and a bad thing to do if you don't, and an easy thing to do if you know how, and a hard thing to do if you don't.

Let's take a look, first of all, at what slanting actually means. To slant a story means to try to increase its chances of salability by studying published stories of the same type in magazines at which you're aiming, and then writing yours in the same general way.

Considered in that manner, slanting makes good sense. Published stories, the stories actually bought and used, are, after all, the best available answer to the question of what the editor wants—and you can increase the chances that yours will be what he wants, too, by studying the accepted stories and patterning yours, in moderation, along the same lines. You know the general type of story you want to write, and you know generally how to plan and plot and write it (or, let us hope, you will when you have finished reading this book), but study of published stories will provide you with necessary additional specific market information: for example, the amount of fast action desired, or whether long love scenes or short ones are preferred, or which delicate subjects they don't seem to mind and which they always seem to avoid.

It is only when the writer goes overboard on the subject of slanting, or slants in the wrong way, that trouble sets in. Let's examine the pitfalls:

1. One much-discussed method of slanting, and one which most experienced writers avoid like a plague, is the blueprinting system. Avoid it, too; it's bad medicine.

The blueprinting method requires the writer to take a published story of the same type as the one he plans to do, and make up a diagram of the story's separate components. You show on your list or diagram, in other words, the exact lines or paragraphs in which the hero and heroine and villain and other characters first enter the story, and the exact lines or paragraphs in which the problem and complications and crisis and solution turn up. And then you write *your* story with exactly the same blueprint, but with your own plot: you have your characters enter the story at exactly or approximately the same points, and you have the problem and complications and crisis and solution happen at exactly or approximately the same points. That is the blueprinting method in essence; some new writers make it even more imitative by ringing in dialogue and description where the published story did.

There's a legend around the field about an editor who received a manuscript which blueprinted a published story so closely that the two were almost identical, but bought it anyway because "at least it shows that the writer is trying to get my slant." Perhaps this legend is true; all I can offer in evidence to the contrary is the fact that every editor I know does nothing with obviously blueprinted stories but reject them. Aside from the fact that too-closely-blueprinted stories smell mightily like plagiarism, most blueprinted stories are rejected because they're contrived messes.

Every story ever written is a little different from every other story ever written. Even where two stories are very similar in theme or problem and solution, some of the characters are bound to be different in some of their actions, and some of the minor or major story events are bound to be different. It's ridiculous to try to force your story into the restriction of another story's exact (or even similar) details of movement: like putting on a size twenty-eight suit when your size is forty, just because the size twenty-eight looked good on another fellow.

2. Furthermore, as pointed out earlier in the book, the story you may choose as your blueprint or guide may be the one yarn in the issue which the editor bought under presssure and which he thinks is terrible. As a general rule, don't ever think you are properly gauging the slant of a magazine or field when you read and study one particular story, no matter how hard you study it and weigh and consider each of its details. You get the slant of a field by reading issue after issue after issue. The details which remain in your mind as recurrent and typical are the important ones.

3. Remember, however, that this point of recurrence and typicalness refers to the general *kinds* of themes and handling and motivation preferred by the magazines in the field, and does not mean that you can get by with near carbon copies of already-published stories. Some new writers slant their stuff so religiously, and pay so much attention to getting their stories exactly like previously published yarns that they are too much like them. They forget all about originality and come up with stories which are complete composites of published material, with nothing new added at all.

A while ago an editor showed me several manuscripts in his brief case, glaring at them as he did so. "The writer who sent these wrote that they're typical slick family-problem stories," he said. "Curiously enough, he's quite right—but they're so darned similar to stuff we've already published that they're going back today. There isn't a fresh breath of air in any of them."

Most editors want, as writer Charles Handley puts it, stories which are "differently the same." Light love stories, family-problem stories, detective stories, and most of the other basic types certainly contain basic similarities in all of their versions, good and bad, but nearly all of the published ones manage to include a fresh angle or a fresh twist. Make sure of that when you're writing. Don't let slanting go so much to your head that you're actually not writing your own stories as much as you are adding a little of your own stuff to composites of other people's stories.

4. Too specific slanting of any kind is dangerous. It is a good idea to slant a story toward one particular magazine only when that magazine is the only one of its kind in the field; otherwise, it's better business to slant generally toward all of the magazines in that field.

All magazines in the slick field, for example, use light love stories—there isn't a single magazine in the field which does not. Only one or two of the magazines in the field, however, use a rather unusual type called the "business story"—a story which contains a good, strong plot and all the other necessary dramatic elements, but which takes place within a specific business or industry, and which gives you so many incidental details on the business operations that you secure an education on the industry along with the story action. If, therefore, you write a light love story, it has a chance of selling all over the field; but if you write a business story slanted for one particular magazine, your chances of sale elsewhere, provided the story does not place at that market for some reason, are extremely tiny or nonexistent.

Many magazines run certain special kinds of stories, or stories with special emphasis on some factor—such as Americana stories, which give extraheavy attention to descriptions of locale and background, or certain types of humorous regional stories. You've undoubtedly seen stories in a magazine which are peculiar to that magazine, more typical of that magazine than of any other in the field. All of the slick magazines, however, and all magazines in other fields—with only the rarest of exceptions—use these special "exclusive" yarns far less often than interchangeable stories: stories which could sell as easily to other magazines in the field as to theirs. You're far safer writing interchangeable stories, at least until you've become so well established that almost everything you write sells at first submission.

Slanting is always done best when it is done intuitively rather than deliberately, when you aren't trying to force your slanting, but are getting the slant into the story because you're filled with the "feel" of the field. And there's only one way, really, that that can be accomplished.

First of all, read all the magazines in your chosen field regularly, with particular attention to your kind of stories in those magazines. Don't ever miss an issue and don't ever skip a story. Read those magazines until the stuff comes out of your ears— read them until you're pretty nearly the world's foremost authority on your chosen field and kind of story and their particular characteristics—read them until it becomes second nature to write your stuff that way. And then go right on reading them.

Don't do much more with those stories than read them, either. It's perfectly all right to read them carefully, and take note of the manner in which the author achieves emotional effects, and the way he introduces his problem, and the other examples of his technical skill, but skip the juggling tricks— the charts and the blueprints and the scissoring apart of the story so that you can write the sections in your own way for practice. Let your mind absorb the slant through reading; don't make the business of slanting unnecessarily complicated.

Read the captions under the illustrations, too, and the

blurbs which usher in the story. Remember that they're the editor's come-on spiel, and his packaging. Sometimes blurbs and captions will give you interesting and important insights into what the editor wants in his magazine—and you're the boy or girl whose business it is to supply him with what he wants.

Until that slant becomes second nature, use a little preliminary step before you begin writing each story. After you've worked out your plot, pick up a bunch of magazines and read the stories of the same type as the one you're about to write. Just read them, nothing more, and then toss them aside and begin writing. You'll find that the reading has moved you into the right channel, and that you're slanting right toward the bull's-eye. And it will be your own story, not someone else's.

21

LINCOLN'S MOTHER'S DOCTOR'S DOG: *The title*

The newspapers once published a story about a noted psychologist, and quoted him as saying that the four words which most easily arouse emotion in Americans are Lincoln, mother, doctor, and dog. This news fired the imagination of one young writer, who immediately pounded out a story and topped it with what he proudly described as the most ideal title of all time: *Lincoln's Mother's Doctor's Dog.*

It is not necessary, happily, to go to such extremes to provide ideal titles for your stories. Your titles don't have to make the reader turn emotional handsprings, anyway: all they have to do is be interesting enough to seduce him into reading the story. And that should never be too hard to do, provided you use your good common sense in making your title selections.

The title is an important part of your sales campaign on your story. It is, provided the physical appearance of your manuscript is not so sloppy that it's distracting, the first thing that the editor sees; and, if the story is bought and published, one of the first things the reader examines while he tries to decide whether to read your story or another in the magazine. It must, therefore, always do its job properly.

There are many things which can be wrong with a title. First and foremost in the chamber of horrors is the dull or trite title, which repels rather than attracts the reader because it makes him suspect that the story itself will be just as dull or trite.

Old saws, overworked proverbs, famous quotations from the Bible, very popular song titles—any phrases at all which have become trite through too common usage are sure to make trite titles. You are bound to suspect that a story will be equally stale in language and plot if the author has given it a title like *Time Will Tell, Murder Will Out, The Worm Turns, An Eye for an Eye, A Scream in the Night,* or *Love Thy Neighbor,* and most of the time you will be right.

If you're planning to use a Biblical or literary quotation or some other familiar phrase as the title of your story, don't do so if it is a recognizable cliché. There are usually only two instances when proverbs and sayings and quotations make good titles: when they are familiar enough to be recognized, but not so familiar that they're trite (for example, *The Naked and the Dead*), and when the triteness is canceled out by an amusing or interesting twist.

Robert Benchley, for example, worked quite an amusing book title out of the old saw about the early bird which catches the worm. The proverb itself is ancient and trite enough only to be usable for sewing on samplers: *The Early Bird* would just never do. Instead Benchley called his book *The Early Worm.* (The angle, of course, is that the proverb may prove the wisdom of early rising because only the bird which rises early gets breakfast—but look what happens to the poor worm which gets up early.) Detective-story writers, too, have made quite an art of twisting trite phrases into fresh and interesting titles. To name a few examples: *Let Me Kill You, Sweetheart, The Facts of Death, Dead Ernest, Has Anybody Here Slain Kelly?, Just Around the Coroner, The Quack and the Dead,* and *Grave and a Haircut.*

The grade-school-composition type of title, such as *A Trip to the City* or *A Day in the Country,* misses because it doesn't offer much promise of excitement. Those stories sound as though they will be dull descriptions of the details of that trip or that day—(*We got on the bus and the man stamped our tickets and we saw a lovely bluejay,* etc. etc.)—in which case they lack problems and all the rest, and, of course, aren't stories at all. If, therefore, you're planning to use a title of that sort because the story events *happen* during the trip or during the day in the country, don't do it; you're putting the accent on the wrong syllable. The fact of the trip or the day in the country is the dullest part of the story; make your title concern the interesting events in the yarn. A title like *A Sunny Afternoon* is deadly dull, but a title like Hemingway's *Death in the Afternoon* is not, because it points to a specific and interesting story line.

You can probably, by now, think of other too general titles which give no real promise of a story or that anything interesting will be happening. Here are a few which come to mind: *Day unto Day, Night Falls on Hoboken, Happy Circus Days.*

Titles which are incomprehensible won't do your story much good, either. P. G. Wodehouse, for example, once turned in a book manuscript titled *Money for Jam.* The title had to be changed because anyone unfamiliar with British slang, which means the bulk of American readers, would not know that it means money which is easy to get, or money on which you can count. The publishers changed the title to *Money in the Bank,* which is our slang way of saying the same thing. The same applies to big word titles: it is difficult to conceive of many readers getting excited over a story entitled *The Dolichocephalic Man,* though *The Long-Headed Man,* which means the same thing, sounds odd enough to be intriguing.

Be careful, too, of titles which sound misleading: which sound like one type of story when you are writing another. If, for example, you are doing a college-background love story, in which a hazing occurs where the heroine is locked in a room with a ketchup-stained dummy made to look like a corpse, don't call your story *Murder on the Campus.* In the same way, don't make love sound like a Western, just because it takes place on a dude ranch, by calling it *Blazing Guns,* or a murder yarn (wherein the female corpse is found clutching a bouquet of roses) sound like a love story by calling it *Roses for My Darling.* One famous example occurred when a Raymond Chandler murder mystery was released as a film under the same title as his book: *Farewell, My Lovely.* Apparently the book got by without much trouble because Chandler's by-line and other markings identified it as a mystery, but the film version caused so much confusion among movie-goers that the producers had to yank the prints back and retitle the picture *Murder, My Sweet.* The danger of misleading titles is that the readers who like your type of story but think it's another type may skip it, and readers who like the other type will be annoyed when they read your story and find it isn't the type they thought at all. It isn't absolutely necessary to categorize your story specifically in the title, but make sure the title doesn't make the story seem to fit in the wrong category, either.

The same principle applies to the use of humorous titles for serious stories, and vice versa. You can see that a title like *The Lost Weekend* was perfect for the film and book it adorned—it conveys wonderfully the mood of the story—but try on for size a title like *Gimme a Quick One, Bartender.* This is not as extreme an example as you may think, either: editors receive an enormous number of stories whose titles are exactly opposite in mood. (I'll never forget the time we received a delicate and tender little story about a mother whose son had been hit by a car and had to have both his upper limbs amputated. The author had titled it: *Look, Ma, No Hands.* Now *there's* an extreme example, but it's true.) Watch this, please: the story title should fit the tone as well as the type.

When you select a title, try to choose one which conveys a hint of what the story is about, and of the interesting stuff in the story. Don't, however, give more than a hint: make sure you aren't giving away too much of a story. A while ago, for example, we received a humorous and screwball fantasy from a client—a story about a baseball player who was wonderful at hitting home runs, but was useless when he hit anything other than homers because his feet were so big and heavy that he could never manage to run around the bases without being tagged out. The story wound up when the player applied his simple faith and worked a miracle by growing wings, so the author called it *Wings for Leadfoot Lonkowski*. The title was certainly an interesting enough one to grip the attention of the reader, but, we felt, it was bad because it gave away the solution before the story started. We sent the story along to the editor, anyway, because we had already discussed the plot with him and knew there was no necessity to worry about the spoiling of *his* suspense: but, surely enough, he phoned and made the same point the moment he saw the title. The story appeared under the title of *Leadfoot Wonder*, which is interesting, too, and doesn't give anything away.

If you're writing a story which builds up to the scene where a big explosion occurs, don't call your story *The Big Explosion*, no matter how much you may like the sound of that title, and no matter how much you may think the readers and the editor will like it. No title is so good that it must be used even though it will spoil the story.

On the other hand, of course, steer clear of the other extreme: titles which are so vague or ambiguous or so faintly connected with the story that the reader can't figure out, after he finishes the story, where the title comes in. You've undoubtedly run across a few of those; the titles are interesting enough, but you just can't figure out what the devil they have to do with the stories. I have spent years trying to figure out some like that; it is my uneasy suspicion that the writers just got tired of trying to think up good titles and just stuck on the first three or four words which came to their minds.

One which I did manage to figure out, after much effort, was a story about a woman who had promised her late husband

that she would always remain faithful to his memory, but
started running around with other men before his body had
cooled. The author called the story *Whirling John,* and you will
understand my puzzlement when I tell you that no character
in the story was named John, and nothing or no one in the
story did any whirling. It took a full hour to remember an old
joke I had heard years before.

In the joke, a man named John Smith discovered that he
was dying, and called his wife to his bedside, and made her
promise that she would always remain true to his memory
and never have anything to do with another man. She promised, and he died, and went to heaven, and eventually his best
friend died and went to heaven, too. The friend wanted to
look up old John, and went to St. Peter for help in finding him.
"John Smith, eh?" St. Peter mused. "That's a tough one—we
have a lot of John Smiths up here. Can you tell me anything
else about him?" The friend thought for a while. "Well," the
friend said, "this John Smith told his wife that he'd turn over
in his grave if she was ever unfaithful to him."

"Aha!" said St. Peter, his face lighting up. "You mean *whirling* John Smith!"

It is easy to picture the obscurity of this title for anyone
who had not heard this joke. We asked the author to change
it—as you should if you find yourself about to use an unclear
title.

Two other types, finally, which are best to avoid: the ultra-
arty title (such as *Catch up the Torch from Faltering Hands*)
and the present-tense title (such as *Johnny Brown Saves a
Marriage*). You'll still see them around occasionally, but they've
become unfashionable and unpopular with editors.

Naturally, the use of a poor title on your story is not the
worst thing you can do in this writing business. Editors always have a good supply of blue pencils on hand to change
the titles they don't think are right; and, besides, there have
been dozens of stories and books published under perfectly

foul titles which have done very well, anyhow. In the early stage of the game, however, when the presence of your by-line on a story does not yet automatically signal that the story is a good one, little things are sometimes enough to tip the scales against you. That first bad impression made by a poor title may be just enough to give the editor the subconscious nudge into throwing an almost-but-not-quite-right story into the rejection pile rather than the acceptance pile: it may be just enough to keep a reader from dipping into a story by a name unknown to him, when otherwise he might read and enjoy it and write a glowing letter to the editor. It isn't much more effort to get a good title instead of settling for a bad one, so you might as well do it right.

22

YOUR WAY WITH WORDS: *Style*

You have noted, as we've discussed one point after another, that there are many things to worry about in this writing business. Well, the development of your own style is not one of them.

There's only, to misquote Samuel Goldwyn, one thing you have to do to develop an individual style: nothing. Your writing style is like your mouth—it grows and shapes itself in the normal course of everyday living.

The factors which mold a man's writing style are the same factors which make him want to write. Heredity enters into it, and childhood reading, and adult reading, and the modes of speech and other influences of the people around him throughout his life. All of these things affect each writer somewhat differently, and give him a style as definitely his own as his fingerprints.

As a result, you don't ever have to worry about developing a style of your own because, my friend, you've already done so. Inescapably or happily, whichever way you want to look at it, you write the way you write, and I write the way I write, and everybody else writes the way he writes.

It is sometimes, or perhaps even usually, rather difficult to realize this fact about your own stuff. You're a little too close to all the trees to see the forest: your own way of thinking is so much a natural part of you, and the words and sentences you use seem such inevitable selections, that it is hard to realize that your own particular personality and background are directing you and causing you to choose words and sentences and language a little or a lot differently from anybody else. You're so closely and personally and mentally tied up with the birth of your stories and with the processes of their manufacture that, though they may look mighty good to you, you'll rarely be able to discern personally the distinguishing trademarks.

Not so an objective reader, however: let him read enough of your stuff so that he's genuinely familiar with it, and he'll be able to spot one of your new yarns at thirty paces, even if it is signed with the by-line of W. Somerset Maugham or George Washington or Genghis Khan. This discovery is usually a little startling to me about my own work, too. I say or write things in the way I do because they seem at the time to be the best way—or at least a good way—to say or write them, and not because I'm making any particular or conscious effort to sound like myself or different from anyone else: yet people often write me after the appearance of my articles on technique in the writers' trade magazines, or the appearance of my other stuff elsewhere, and tell me they liked my style or they knew *I* was writing the moment they scanned the page. This information is pleasant to hear, but it's surprising, because, as I say, it's difficult to conceive that you automatically sound a little different from everybody else. In the same way, many of the several hundred writers my agency represents may believe, no doubt, that their styles are not especially distinctive, yet it is my solemn boast (which I prove regularly) that I can read several unsigned pages of manuscript by any of them and tell at once whose work it is.

Naturally, there are some writers whose works are more heavily stylized than others. Among present-day writers—and writers of all time, for that matter—there are some whose styles pop right out at you the first time you read their stuff, whose styles are so different or unusual or bizarre that you are always conscious of them. Usually these styles are artificial, deliberately created by the author for their own effect, and sometimes they enhance a story and make it more interesting. More often, however, they have the failing of being so bizarre and attention-grasping that they distract the reader from the story line: and, therefore, most professional writers prefer to use their own natural styles, which are distinctive enough naturally to trademark their stories, but not so spectacularly different that the reader is continually reminded that he is reading.

You must remember that the primary function of your writing style is communication, the job of communicating the story to the reader in the clearest and least distracting way. The differences in natural style result from the differences in language used by each writer to express and communicate the story events to the reader, and to make the reader feel the proper emotions as the story events are told. When the style goes beyond the purpose of communication—when it is so visible in itself that it steadily takes the reader's attention away from the story events—it is usually not doing its job properly.

There is a reporter's anecdote which seems to me to express very clearly the error of becoming so conscious of your pretty style that you forget that your real job is to tell a story. It concerns a city editor who found himself short-staffed when the Johnstown flood suddenly occurred, and had to send a raw new cub to cover it.

After many hours of nervous waiting, the cub's coverage wire was finally received. It was about five thousand words long, contained practically no facts, and was expressed throughout exactly like its opening sentence: "God sits tonight in judgment at Johnstown."

Curtly, the editor wired back. "Forget flood; interview God."

Fiction stories, of course, are rarely the same kinds of bare statements of fact as newspaper stories. Your style must embellish the facts and round them out and make them interesting and dramatic, but not at the expense of the facts.

I believe that it was Dickens who said that the thing to do with the outstanding phrases and sentences in your stories is strike them out. In moderation, that is good advice. It is a little extreme because I believe no writer in the world can resist sticking in a good phrase or line when he happens to think of one, and, besides, occasional outstanding lines spice up the story and don't distract too much. When, however, every stay at the typewriter is a constant struggle to achieve a beautiful style, and when you find yourself leaning over backward to make every sentence a thing of beauty and a joy forever, it is time to realize that you're overdoing it. Just concentrate on telling your story; your good style will take care of itself, without becoming too much of a good thing.

Overwriting of any kind is bad stuff. The effect is always distracting when you use six adjectives where one would do, or when you use too many poetic words (*the man's feral eyes gleamed as he looked at the gibbous moon*), or when you describe a character's reactions to a situation in such great and exaggerated detail that the effect becomes ludicrous. The current technique as far as the latter is concerned, as a matter of fact, is to *underplay* very dramatic scenes.

This term, borrowed from the theatre, is the difference between the old-style actor's method of depicting emotion and the new-style actor's manner of doing the same thing. The old-style actor tears at his hair, screams and groans, wrinkles his face into a thousand creases to show grief; the new-style actor shows the same thing, and many times more effectively, by standing still and rigid with shock, a look of slow horror creeping onto his face. In a story, the old, overwritten style was to describe an emotion like grief by going into great and wordy detail; today, authors show the same emotion far more effectively by hinting at it, by suggesting it so delicately that the reader's imagination goes to work and makes him see it all the more clearly.

There is an example of this in the Western story about the blind man, previously discussed. To gain sympathy for the blind man's feeling of uselessness, particularly in a setting like the Old West, where physical prowess and physical capabilities are so important, you could easily overwrite the scene by giving the blind man a long, tear-jerking speech about his condition, and how he can't get work, and how nobody cares a damn about him, and so on far into the night. The author of the story underplays it with a single line which is much more effective.

"Us blind fellows ain't kept too busy, Lorna," he said softly.

It seems to me that there is hopelessness reflected in that sentence; it seems to me that it sums up a great deal of sadness without a lot of overwritten ballyhoo.

In humorous stories, Wodehouse is a master at the art of underplaying scenes. Supposing you were describing a discussion between two men, in which one is a tough egg, and the other is badly scared. You can easily overwrite it by giving an overlong description of the frightened man's white face, the perspiration on his palms, the way he runs his finger around his collar. Wodehouse underplays it by merely suggesting it:

He flicked the ash from his cigar. I did not need to do it to mine.

Again, here is Wodehouse, underplaying in describing a man's reactions at being faced by a hunting rifle:

The fascination of shooting as a sport depends almost wholly on whether you are on the right or the wrong end of the gun.

For an excellent example of underplaying and understatement which greatly increases the effectiveness and emotional pitch of a story, I refer you to Stephen Vincent Benét's *Too Eary Spring*, particularly the concluding lines.

The lack of rhythm in style—too many short sentences or too many long sentences in a row—is almost always an unnatural state resulting from too much worry over getting the proper mixture. Most people think and talk and write in a natural mixture of short and long sentences; you'll always get it if you forget about it and concentrate on telling your story. This will be a bugaboo only if you make it so.

23

". . . AND IN THE BEGINNING . . .": *The opening*

There are three points at which the normal story, told in chronological fashion, can open: just before the problem comes up, just as the problem comes up, and just after the problem has come up. It is important that you make the correct choice as you settle down to write your story.

Let's take a look at the same story opened in each of the three ways. The just-before-the-problem opening first:

They stood there silently in the sunlight for a moment, a couple of kids in love, too full of happiness to speak. Then the church bells began to chime in the village, and Joe Benson grinned ruefully.

"I was hoping those bells would never ring," he said, "but there they are. Five o'clock—and I'd better get home and finish up those organizational charts. How would it look if the new general manager of Townsley and Marshall turned up tomorrow for his first day on the job and didn't have his charts ready?"

Della Lane's lovely young face was solemn. "That would never do," she said. "You've got to make them glad they've given you this opportunity—glad they've allowed a newcomer to buy a partnership in the oldest firm in town. You've got to do everything right."

They walked slowly down the road toward Della's home, hand in hand. "You betcha," Joe said. "Sure would be sad if I got canned on my first day, after I'd invested every nickel I have in the world. Not that they could, of course."

They reached the gate to the house, and kissed with a sort of desperation born of the knowledge that they'd be apart for all of twenty-four hours. Then Joe jumped into his car and drove back to his own house.

The evening paper lay open on his porch, and the headline story made his heart lurch sickeningly within him. It said the treasurer of Townsley and Marshall had absconded with the company funds, and that the firm had collapsed.

I've telescoped this a little for space reasons, of course; the scene can actually run considerably longer before the problem shows up.

Here is the same story opening just as the problem arrives:

The sound of the morning paper thumping on the front porch awoke Joe Benson, and he tumbled out of bed cheerfully, put on a bathrobe, and went down to get it. Life looked mighty bright to him, and he whistled as he walked. Just one more day, and he'd begin work as the new general manager at Townsley and Marshall.

And then he opened the paper, and his dreams crumbled into little pieces and dissolved before his eyes. The headline story said that the treasurer for Townsley and Marshall had absconded with the company funds, and the firm had collapsed.

The newspaper dropped from Benson's fingers. He was wiped out—finished. He had put every nickel he owned in the world into buying a partnership in the firm.

He went to the phone to call Della Lane. . . .

Again somewhat telescoped, but the difference is obvious. The other version makes a preliminary build-up before the problem is sprung; this one springs the problem at once. And here is the same story as it would open after the problem has arrived:

Joe Benson sat numbly for a long while, his fingers crumpling and uncrumpling the morning paper. Finally, he got to his feet, and, like a man walking in his sleep, went over to the phone and dialed Della Lane's number.

Her sweet young voice held a note of banter, "Joe Benson!" she said. "Why aren't you busy working on the organizational report you promised your new partners?"

His voice surprised even him when he replied: it was a harsh, hideous croak. "Haven't you read the morning paper, Della?" he asked.

"Why, no," she said, "not yet. Joe—what's the matter?"

"I'm wiped out," he said dully. "The treasurer at Townsley and Marshall has absconded with the company funds. The firm's--collapsed."

This version, of course, differs from the others because it opens with the problem already on the scene, and with the lead character recovering from his initial shock and about ready to begin action to solve his problem. All three versions, naturally, move through some more building up of the problem—to show why he can't just shoulder his loss and get another job and make more money; to give some reason that it is *urgent* to get his money back—to eventual struggles to solve the problem. The three differ in the degree of rapidity with which the problem is covered and passed and the struggles begun.

All three types of opening are fine, and turn up in equal amounts in the magazines. The matter of choice depends entirely upon the comparative dramatic strength of the opening events.

If you have an idea for an introductory or pre-problem scene which seems to you to do very well the double job of introducing the lead character interestingly while it emphasizes the gravity or blackness of the subsequent problem (by showing the comparative brightness of things *before* the problem arrived), then the pre-problem opening is the one to use. If the arrival of the problem itself seems to you to be more interesting and dramatic than the events immediately preceding it, or than a description of the lead character's postproblem reactions, then the just-as-the-problem-arrives opening is best. And if a description of the lead character's reactions to the problem, or his first move to solve the problem, strikes you as the more dramatic event in the particular story you're planning, then by all means start with the just-after-the-problem-has-come-up opening.

There are dangers attached to each of the three: look out for them. If you use the just-before-the-problem type of opening, don't run the pre-problem scene too long. It may run longer than the example given, but not too much longer; say five hundred words at the absolute outside. The problem is the thing which really grips and holds the reader, and, however interesting the pre-problem scene may be, he won't be willing to wait too long for the trouble to show up.

And if you use the just-as or just-after openings, don't devote so much attention to describing the problem arrival or the post-problem action that you forget all about your lead character. Try to build up a picture of him and of the other important characters, as the examples given began to do. Remember that your reader will be interested in the problem only if he is interested in the character who has it.

Whichever type of opening you choose, try to get all the major characters into the story as close to the opening as possible, preferably within the first five hundred words, and at least in the first quarter of the story. The reader wants to know as intimately as possible the people to whom things happen or who are a part of the things which happen, and it is never satisfactory when a new character pops up late in the story and is the cause or a part of a major story development.

Don't, of course, go to the other extreme either—rush so hard to get your major characters into the story early that you get them all in within the first fifty words, and bewilder the reader the way most people in real life are bewildered when they are introduced to a roomful of people all at once. This sort of thing will never do:

Tom Fowler grinned wryly as he walked into his apartment and almost tripped over a mop and pail. Wasn't that just like Midge, to make such a fuss about keeping things tidy, and then leave everything in the middle of the floor just to run downstairs with Mike and Alice. Well, she'd be back soon, unless she had stopped off afterward to see Eileen, or to have dinner with Slim. And in any case, he had more important things to think about. It was urgent that he phone Sam and Henry and tell them about Arthur, and warn them not to let Jane know.

Introduce your characters as early as possible in the story, but not so very close on the heels of one another that they do not emerge as separate entities. Give the reader just a little breathing space between them, and try to establish, as each character appears, or fairly soon afterward, his relationship to the others.

The use of the narrative hook as the start of any type of opening—just-before, just-as, or just-after—achieved an immense amount of popularity in its heyday, and has now simmered down to the point where it is usable only when greatly modified. For those unfamiliar with this phrase, a narrative hook is a startling or shocking first sentence of a story which hooks the reader and pulls him forcibly into the story.

Let us say, for example, that you open your story with this sentence:

Hank Rogers walked over to a dark corner and, stealthily, changed heads.

That is a narrative hook: it is certainly sufficiently startling that the reader will read on just to find out what the heck is meant—how a man can possibly change his head. And even when the reader learns that the scene is a masquerade ball, and Rogers has just substituted the papier-mâché head for another, he will, presumably, go on reading.

The narrative hook in its original one-startling-sentence form died a fairly rapid death, or at least sank quickly into severe paralysis, for two reasons: overuse and general crudity. After all, if you see story after story after story after story with narrative hooks of that type, each shocker vying to outshock all the other shockers, you reach the point where an opening sentence is startling only if it says merely that the day was bright and sunny.

Modified, the narrative hook is still a good idea; anything which pulls the reader into the story is good. A provocative sentence, for example, will often work the trick:

Judy always arrived early at the station so she could get a seat in the first car.

There's nothing particularly shocking or startling about this —which, for the reasons given, is fine—but it *is* interesting. Why, the reader wonders, is it so important that she get a seat in the *first* car—and he reads on.

You are also on the beam when you consider your opening scene or first few scenes as a narrative hook, because, after all, the purpose of the beginning of your story is to hook and interest your reader into reading the rest of the story. You're flirting with triteness and crudity when you employ the narrative hook in its narrowest interpretation, meaning *only* a startling opening and *only* in the first or first few sentences. In its broad interpretation, however—as the fact that your general opening should interest and hook the reader and pull him into the story—it is a good point, even an essential point.

For an excellent example of a narrative hook which occupies an entire chapter of a book, I refer you to the first chapter of the Craig Rice mystery novel, *Eight Faces at Three.* You'll find it difficult to prevent yourself from reading the remaining chapters after you've read this first one.

One other type of opening device which has gone almost entirely out of fashion is the dialogue opening, of which the following is an example:

"Look—there it comes again."

Ray Latimer shouted these words as he watched the small red airplane buzzing the house down the road.

Overuse has killed this one, too: it was such a standard opener in most books written around the turn of the century that it looks more than a little old-fashioned today. Most current editors dislike it, and a few even consider it a downright taboo. You'd better let it molder in its grave.

24

QUOTE, END QUOTE: *Dialogue*

The difference between dialogue in real life and dialogue in fiction is that fiction dialogue must have point and destination. It can never be merely general or polite conversation.

In real life, two men can meet on a street corner and talk for an hour without saying anything of importance to the lives of either of them. In real life, two men can meet for an important conference and spend an hour in general conversation before they get down to the important items. The funds in real life of how-are-you, how's-the-wife, nice-weather-we're-having, ever-hear-the-one-about, and all the rest are inexhaustible. In fiction, however, every line in the story must move and advance it toward its inevitable destination, and dialogue must do its part.

All fiction, when you stop to consider it, does not reflect life exactly as it happens, but, rather, gives a picture of faster-moving and more directly moving life by condensing and high-lighting. When you plot a story, you use a series of events which could conceivably happen in real life (or, if you're doing a fantasy, a series of events which could conceivably happen in real life provided that the basic fantastic concept were true), but you're actually condensing and highlighting life by using only events directly related to the situation—and leaving out unrelated events, and all the casual meetings with persons unrelated to the events, and descriptions of all the mechanics of everyday living (three meals a day, toothbrushing, hair combing, etc.). When you're describing a character or locale in a story, you don't describe every detail; you condense and highlight by giving just enough of the important facts to build an accurate picture. And when you use dialogue, you condense and highlight by using only essential and related conversation —conversation which advances the plot directly by adding new information, or indirectly by giving a clearer picture of the characters or their relationships to each other.

Fiction conversation, then, is real-life conversation without its sidetracks or its traditional opening gambits, or at least without most of them. It is the meat, the substance, of real-life conversation, with a little general or unrelated conversation added only when necessary to achieve a more realistic effect.

You've undoubtedly seen a great many loan requests handled this way in fiction:

> The bell rang, and Jerry walked over and opened the door. Martin burst into the room.
> "Jerry," he said, "you've got to help me. They're going to throw me out of my apartment if I don't pay my rent by three o'clock. You've got to let me have a hundred bucks until Thursday."

However urgent the need, few real-life conversations approach the point so directly. In real life, the doorbell will ring, and Jerry will walk over and ask who it is, and Martin will answer, and Jerry will say, "Well, for Pete's sake—of all people," and he'll open the door and they'll shake hands. And Jerry will call his wife and say, "Look who's here," and Martin will ask Jerry's wife how she is and ask Jerry how he is, and Jerry's wife and Jerry will ask Martin how he is and how his wife is, and they'll discuss the state of health of their children, and discuss the last time they saw each other and what they've been doing since then, and the conversation will circle around and around a while longer until Martin comes to the request for the money —the only part of the conversation, if it were fiction, in which the reader will really be interested.

The loan-request example, of course, is conversation at top speed to point up Martin's excitement and the urgency of the request. It can also be handled more slowly:

> The bell rang, and Jerry walked over to the door.
> "Yes?" he said. He pulled the door open when the caller replied. "Well, what do you know?" he said. "Martin Sloane!"
> Sloane stepped into the room. "Hello, Jerry," he said. "It's nice to see you again."
> "Nice to see you, too," Jerry said. "What brings you out to this part of town?"
> Sloane hesitated for a moment. "It's this way, Jerry," he said slowly. "I'm in trouble—thought maybe you could help me out. They're going to throw me out of my apartment if I don't pay my rent by three o'clock." His voice quickened, became desperate. "You've got to let me have a hundred bucks until Thursday."

Here the point is reached more slowly, and something of Martin Sloane's natural embarrassment is shown, but this stretch of dialogue is still considerably more sped up and condensed than real-life conversation. It sums up this way: much real-life conversation is aimless and pointless, and aimlessness and pointlessness in fiction just won't hold readers. You should no more include unessential and uninteresting dialogue than you should include unnecessary scenes or events which have nothing else to do with the story.

Don't, of course, slide to the other extreme, and run your conversations like this:

> The bell rang, and Jerry walked over and opened the door. Martin burst into the room.
> "Getting tossed out of my room unless I pay rent by three—gimme a hundred till Thursday."

You don't have to make your characters talk like telegrams in order to leave out unessentials. Make your story conversations as normal-sounding and realistic as possible, but leave out most of the frills usually found in real-life conversations.

Comparatively few stories sell which contain less than 20 per cent dialogue, and unquestionably a goodly amount of dialogue in a story sits well with the readers. You've probably seen people flip through the pages of a story or book and gauge the amount of dialogue when deciding whether or not to read it, because stories with lots of dialogue are usually easier and more pleasant to read than those with long stretches of unbroken narration. Dialogue, however, must never be included for the sole sake of having a lot of it; like all other fiction ingredients, it must do its part to keep the story moving along.

Just as one big chunk of narrative can become boring, incidentally, so can one big chunk of dialogue—a long speech from one person. When a long speech is necessary, try to break it up by insertions of dialogue from other persons. You want to avoid, wherever possible, any unbroken stretches in your story —page-long paragraphs of narrative or dialogue. Explanations usually suffer from this fault, and here is how one such speech, which would otherwise run too long unrelieved and without a break, might be broken up:

Mike turned and looked at Amy.

"You're the killer, Amy," he said. "You hated Rosalie because she took a new-look haircut before you did, and because she stole Joe away from you. You had access to the poison because everybody knows that your hobby is collecting rare old drugs. You went over to her house the night she was leaving for Cincinnati for the weekend, hid in the dumbwaiter until the place was empty, and then sneaked in and put poison in all her reducing pills. Then you made sure that she'd take a pill soon by asking her when she came back if she didn't think she'd gained a little weight."

Amy didn't look sweet and innocent any more. Her fingers twisted into claws, and she said viciously, "You're out of your mind."

Mike shook his head. "No," he said, "maybe it's just that I'm sane for the first time in months. You were the one who shot Hiram, too, when you felt he was getting too close to the truth. I wondered why you were wearing a coat that warm summer day we met just outside the old barn. You had put it on because there were blood-stains all over your blouse. . . ."

Sergeant Summers cut in hoarsely, "I hope you can prove all this, Mike."

"Don't worry about it," Mike said. "I can prove everything. I can also prove that, when Hiram didn't die from the bullet wounds . . ."

You can see where Mike's explanation would total up to quite a big chunk if Amy and Summers had not cut in. Whenever a character must make a long speech in a story, interrupt him every once in a while. If he's talking, he's talking to some-body; have that somebody chip in with a few words at logical moments. Or, if he's making a banquet speech or something of that sort, where you find it difficult to interrupt him with dialogue by another character, have him interrupt himself to take a drink of water, clear his throat, point to someone, or something of that sort.

Indirect dialogue, where you tell rather than show the reader what the characters are saying, is usually a poor bet because you're passing up a logical opportunity to get some more "live" dialogue into your story. Here is an example of indirect dia-logue:

He told her that he loved her and that it was silly for them to live apart any longer, and she said that she felt the same way.

This sort of thing turns up in new writers' manuscripts quite often, and it is downright foolish. For no logical reason, it passes up a legitimate opportunity for dialogue by covering the conversation in a far less dramatic way. Don't do it.

There are three instances in which indirect dialogue should be used. One is where you are running a long stretch of con-versation between characters, and feel that a brief pause for indirect dialogue for a few lines will be a refreshing break.

Choose, of course, the least important part of the conversation to do that. Another is where a piece of conversation must be recorded in the story, but where the exact conversation is not important or interesting enough to be given in detail. (For example: *He told him exactly how to operate the pressing machine.*) And the third is where a piece of action or conversation which has already occurred in the story is later described to another character. (For example: *He met Joan on the way back from the fire, and told her about how Sam had rushed in and saved the Smith kid.*)

Aside from these three instances, use direct dialogue in preference to indirect every time. The more "live" dialogue you get into your stories, provided it is always relevant, the better.

When you use dialogue, make sure that, aside from the fact that it is condensed, it always sounds natural—the way people really talk.

Don't ever, for example, make dialogue unnatural just to convey a fact to the reader. Very often in inexpert stories, one character will say something like this to another character: "I saw your father, John H. Collins, on the street the other day." Obviously, the author's purpose is to tell the reader the father's full name, because it will later be important in the story—but after all! People just don't talk that way: the latter character knows his father's full name, and it's doubtful that he has such a variety of fathers that specific identification is necessary. If a fact of this sort is necessary to the story, it must be brought out in more logical and natural fashion: for example:

"I saw your father on the street the other day, Collins," Joe said.
"Gosh, I haven't been over to visit him in months," Collins said. "How did old John H. look? Pretty chipper, I'll bet."

And remember when you are writing dialogue that people don't talk like written matter or as though they've been rehearsing their lines. I have seen a great many unpublished manuscripts which contain passages like the following:

"I walked over to the window to examine the jewelry display, Joe," Frank said. "Going to the side of the window, I saw that the big pendant was missing."

The latter sentence is unnatural because it is what you might call a typical written rather than spoken sentence; people rarely part their sentences in formal ways in normal, unrehearsed speech. Say it aloud, and you'll see what I mean: it has too planned and too narrative a tone about it. The same, of course, applies to other sentences of the kind.

It is a good idea, incidentally, particularly when you are starting out in the writing business, to say aloud any bits of dialogue which seem suspect to you. If they sound unnatural or stiff, discard them. When you become more experienced, your mind's ear will begin to reject unsuitable dialogue automatically.

If you worry a lot about thinking up substitutes for "said," make a simple little experiment. Select a half-dozen stories in current magazines, and make a tally of the amount of times they use "said," and the amount of times they use substitutes. You'll find, perhaps to your surprise, that substitutes are used less than 10 per cent of the time.

The business of worrying over substitutes for "said" is a pretty foolish one, because there doesn't happen to be anything wrong with "said" itself. The purpose of the word and its myriad substitutes is to identify the person doing the speaking, and there's really no reason to get fancy about it. It is the things which are *being* said which count, not the means of tying the speech to the speaker.

Nearly all of the time, the word "said" itself—and its several plain and simple brothers, such as "asked," "replied," "shouted," etc.—will do the job quite adequately; or, if an emotion must be shown and the dialogue doesn't accomplish this completely, a simple descriptive word can be added, such as "said angrily" or "said bitterly" or "said coldly." Once in a while, a more colorful word is needed, such as "screeched" or "spat" or "howled."

But the constant hunt for substitutes for "said"—the avoidance of this best word and the steady substitution of "reiterated," "observed," "conjectured," "ejaculated," and others of the same clan—does far more harm than good. The word which ties up speaker-identification is supposed to do so in a quiet and unobtrusive manner. Constant variation and use of too big words fails in its purpose because it becomes a distraction in itself.

Another thing which need not be worried about is the trick of splitting up dialogue in unusual manners for variety. Here is a sentence split up in the normal manner:

"I'm going to take you home," said Jim.

Here is the sentence split up in an unusual manner:

"I'm going," said Jim, "to take you home."

Or even, in its more consciously cute version:

"I'm going to take," said Jim, "you home."

The unusual split in dialogue enjoyed a brief flurry of popularity in the slicks, but, like all abnormal devices, it was quickly overused and its popularity has now almost completely faded. When you write the sections of dialogue in your stories, you'll note points at which the "he saids" obviously belong. Be smart: put them there.

In writing long stretches of conversation between two characters, by the way, it is all right to leave out identifying phrases for short stretches because the reader can figure out when Character A is talking and when Character B is talking by the order of their remarks. Get in your "A said" and "B said" every four remarks or so, however, or your reader may become confused and wonder why the villain is suddenly saying, "Don't you dare kiss me, you brute," and the heroine is answering, "Scream all you want—no one can hear you."

One mechanical point: when a stretch of dialogue by a single character is a long one and occupies more than one paragraph, leave out the quotation marks at the end of all paragraphs but the last one. That will identify the whole section as his speech. Here is an example:

"Well," said Joe, "this thing happened to me when I was just a boy. I decided to play hooky one day, and went to the local burlesque show instead. It was there that I met Maisie.

"Maisie was playing hooky from school, too—she was a senior at the Haven for Delinquent Girls—and I fell for her immediately. Maybe it was the obvious purity of her soul, and maybe it was—well, let it go. Anyhow, we saw each other every night after that.

"After we'd been going together for a few months . . ."

It is best, of course, as I have said, to interrupt long speeches, but that is the way to do it if you cannot manage to work in interruptions.

Most editors today don't like dialect. They feel that it often offends readers of the same race or nationality, and they feel that it is usually hard to follow and therefore disliked by most readers.

It is about 95 per cent impossible to sell a story told entirely in dialect, and your best bet is to avoid dialect altogether. If you *must* use a dialect-speaking character, try to skip showing dialect through misspelled words (for example: *"Yess, ve haff got goot fresh cake today"*) and do it through the easier-to-read method of using correctly spelled words plus the occasional addition of a few familiar words in the foreign tongue (for example, "Ja, *we have fresh* strudel *today*"). That will often do the trick, and you'll have a much better chance of securing the editorial nod.

25

OVER THE RIVER AND THROUGH THE WOODS:
Transition

This is going to be one of the shortest chapters in the book, because the technique of transition is simplicity itself. It is an important subject because a great many writers do it wrong, but you'll have no trouble with it once you understand the simple principles.

Transition is the act of changing from one scene to another, or moving your characters from one place or time to another. Let's cut in at the tail end of a scene and have a look at transition done badly:

. . . Keller glared. "Don't be a damned fool, O'Leary. I must have those plans today."

"And I'll tell you once again that I'm sorry," O'Leary said. "I have strict orders to give the plans to no one but Professor Masters."

"Will five hundred dollars make you forget your orders? It isn't as though you'll be doing anything illegal. . . ."

"You won't get these plans for five million dollars." O'Leary turned his back and looked down at his desk.

Keller stood there impotently for a moment. Then he shrugged and stalked out of the door.

He walked down the corridor to the elevator, waited until it arrived, entered, and rode down the ten floors to the street level. He walked out of the building, went down the corner to wait for a street car, boarded one, and rode the mile and a half to the center of town.

He got off in front of Police Headquarters, a squat and square red-brick building, and hurried up the stairs to the main entrance. He confronted the sergeant at the desk.

"I'd like to see the chief of detectives," he said.

He had to tell the entire story to the sergeant, and then again to several other officers. Finally, after almost a half hour, he was ushered in to see Chief of Detectives Charles Arlen.

"I want to swear out a warrant for Terence O'Leary of State University," Keller said. "He's stolen some important plans from me. . . ."

The pause that depresses in this sequence is the transition section: the detailed description of Keller's movements between the end of one scene (which closes when Keller stalks out of O'Leary's office) and the beginning of the next scene (which actually starts with the first pieces of important action —Keller's talk with Arlen). The reader's interest lies in the scenes in which things vital to the plot occur; he neither requires nor is much interested in step-by-step accounts of the movement between these scenes.

Here is how the transition should be handled to eliminate the unimportant and dull details of the movements between scenes:

". . . You won't get these plans for five million dollars." O'Leary turned his back and looked down at his desk.

Keller stood there impotently for a moment. Then he turned and stalked out of the room.

A half hour later Keller sat in front of a wide, scarred desk and faced Chief of Detectives Charles Arlen.

"You want to make a formal complaint against this man O'Leary?" Arlen asked.

"You bet I do," Keller said. "He stole my plans, and I want him arrested and the plans returned to me today."

The moment a scene has ended, which means the moment the last piece of important action in the scene has been shown, it is the author's job to close the scene as quickly as possible, and move as quickly as possible to the important action in the next scene. The details of transition do nothing for the story but slow it up and create an unnecessary pause between important action. It is wise to avoid them by closing a scene the moment the last piece of important action has been shown, skipping four single spaces to denote a change of scene or passage of time, and starting right up with the first important piece of action in the new scene. The four-space skip is the automatic sign today that the scene is changing: once asterisks (***) used to do the job, but they are now considered old-fashioned.

When it is possible to change scenes with a movement description of one line or so—for example: *He walked across the street and stopped in at the lingerie store to see Diana*—it is all right to do that instead of the four-space skip. It is when the details of transition take too long, boringly long, that they are bad. Your reader rarely has to be told that the character has driven or taken a trolley to his next destination, and other such routine things; he'll assume that the character has used the normal means of transportation and not flapped his arm and flown through the air.

Sometimes transition to a new scene can be made even smoother by closing the old one with a hint or statement about the character's next stop. The example given might do that in this way:

. . . "You won't get these plans for five million dollars." O'Leary turned his back and looked down at his desk.

Keller stood there impotently for a moment. "All right," he said finally. "Then I'll get the plans in another way. I'll tell the police that you stole them from me."

Chief of Detectives Charles Arlen handed Keller a fountain pen and a printed form.

"Sign this formal complaint at the bottom, please," he said. "It'll enable us to issue a warrant and pick up O'Leary."

Here is another example which names both the time and place of the next scene:

Armstrong scooped up his hat and walked to the door. "That seems to do it for today," he said. "Don't forget to meet me at the Lakeside Inn tomorrow at nine."
"I'll be there," Jim said.

He arrived at the Inn right on time, but Armstrong was nowhere around.

Simple enough, you'll agree.

Most editors today, incidentally, prefer that short stories confine their total scope of action to fairly short periods of time and fairly small areas. They don't generally like short stories in which the action covers a period like twenty or thirty years, or where the stories skip from scene to scene all around the world; they prefer, usually, that the entire story take place in a maximum period of a few weeks or a month (except, as discussed, for necessary flashbacks into the past), and all in one town, or perhaps two at the most. Novelettes, serials, and novels, of course, can cover entire lifetimes or even eras if necessary, and move all around the world and back home again.

26

STUFFING THE HOLLOW MAN: *Characterization*

My dictionary defines character as the sum total of all the qualities which distinguish a person from others. Characterization in fiction, then, to follow this lead, is the method of distinguishing your story people from one another—and thereby enabling your reader to know and understand them better and see them more clearly—by revealing their individual and distinctive qualities or "nature."

It is no longer acceptable to characterize a story person, to distinguish him from all the others in the story, by tacking a simple label on him—in other words, by coming right out and calling him greedy, or mean, or good-hearted, or bad-tempered, or villainous, or anything of that sort. That was all right in the earlier period when, as we have discussed, readers were apparently more trusting, but it is not all right now. Today's readers all seem to hail, at least in spirit, from Missouri: they want to be shown. They're unwilling to accept the author's unbacked-up word for the nature or character of the story people: they want to be shown the inner workings of each of them and be allowed to draw their own conclusions.

The means of demonstrating the characters of your story people are exactly the same as the means by which the characters of real-life people are demonstrated to you in everyday living. How, after all, are you able to gauge and evaluate the

inner workings of people around you, and eventually understand their characters and know them for what they are?
You do so through your observation of three types of outward
signs: the things they do, the way they act when things happen
to them, and their obvious reasons for doing things. To put it
another way, you judge people by their actions, reactions, and
motivations.

Let us say, for example, that you are walking down the
street with an acquaintance, and he stops to buy a magazine
at a corner stand operated by a shabby old blind man, counts
his change, and hurries you away, and then shows you, at a
safe distance, that he has been given an extra quarter by mistake. You don't have to look for a sign on his back, or get an
X-ray and peer inside him, to become aware that he is mean
and without pity; his action in not returning the coin to the old
blind man has shown you that.

Or, if I may address this to the young ladies for a moment,
let us say that you are being visited by a new boy friend, and
a large mouse suddenly runs around the room. You look round,
expecting the boy friend to shoo the mouse away, and there
he is standing on the cocktail table with his trousers pulled up
above his knees. You don't need his horoscope to show you
that he is cowardly; his reactions to the mouse situation have
told you that.

And if a man comes to you and tells you a story about the
dubious morals of a mutual acquaintance, and you know the
story to be absolutely untrue, and realize that it is being told
only because the speaker resents the mutual acquaintance's
success and hopes to injure him, you know at once that the
speaker is a tremendously jealous type. You have been made
aware of it by his obvious motivation of extreme jealousy.

Sometimes, as in the examples given, you are able to tab a
person's character, or a strong phase of his character, accurately
on the basis of a single occurrence, sometimes a lot of things
must occur before you can add them up and know him for

what he is. However rapidly or slowly you can reach your conclusion, at any rate, it always comes, since you are not a mind reader, from one or a combination of the three outward signs—actions, reactions, motivations.

I believe you can easily see, from the examples given and from others in real life which will occur to you, why the newer method of characterizing by showing the reader is so much better and more satisfying than the old one of just telling him. When someone characterizes another person—tells you the other person is a swell guy or a louse, or a coward or exceptionally brave, and so on—you may believe him or you may not; most of the time, if you are a person of good sense and fairness yourself, you will reserve judgment until you are able to observe the fellow and form your own opinion. When, however, you see that person in action and form an opinion yourself, you know that the opinion is altogether correct (at least as far as you're concerned), because, by gosh, you've seen for yourself. The show-the-reader method of characterization allows the reader to see for himself and be convinced.

It is not necessary to characterize all the people, major and minor, in your stories. Who cares if the Western Union messenger who delivers a telegram to the hero on page 3 and never turns up in the story again is a greedy little runt and kicks about his tip and asks for more? Who cares if the cop from whom the hero asks directions on page 9 is a mean and evil-tempered old bird who gives the information grudgingly? You *may* give some of your minor story people quick little characterizations if you want to add occasional humorous or realistic touches, but the point is that it is not essential that you do so all or even most of the time: the minor characters play so unimportant a part in the story, and appear in the story so briefly, that it isn't necessary for the reader to know and understand them and see them clearly. Several editors, as a matter of fact, go whole hog on the subject of unimportance of minor characters, and even send back for revision any otherwise satisfactory stories in which too much space and attention is given to characterization and physical descriptions of minor story people. They feel that too heavy focus on the unimportant people, while they are on stage performing their unimportant action, is an unnecessary distraction from the straight story line, and creates further distraction because the reader believes they are important characters (in view of the amount of attention given them during their appearances on stage) and keeps wondering why they don't come back into the story.

It is vital, however, that all of your major story people be characterized. They must never be a collection of wax dummies, all apparently stamped out of the same mold; they must be distinctly different people with distinctly different personalities so that the reader can form distinct pictures and opinions of each of them.

That does not mean that you must necessarily differentiate between them by giving them such odd or outstanding characteristics that the *dramatis personae* of your stories look like the membership of the local booby hatch. You can, without question, think of four or five young men in your town who are of the same general background—all likable, all of approximately the same cultural and educational level, and no sneaks, meanies, abnormally jealous individuals, or cowards among them—and yet each one's personality is obviously and recognizably distinct and different from all the others. The answer lies in their manner or style, and in their exact approach and attitude toward everything—the sum total of the *smaller* differences in their general actions, reactions, and motivations.

Two of them, for example, may like the same girl—and, though they may be of the same type generally, their approach to the courtship of the girl will immediately make them distinguishable. One, a quiet and less forward type, would take the girl out often, and try to be pleasant and interesting to her, but would not try to overwhelm her in any way. The other, a slicker and faster-moving type, would send her tons of candy, bales of roses, and otherwise try to swamp her into succumbing rapidly.

As characterization in a story, this sort of difference of approach and manner does the job very nicely—for, though neither man possesses extreme characteristics like excessive meanness or cowardice, it is certainly easy to distinguish between them. And when you add the other factors which might mark the difference between a typical slick young fellow and a typical quiet young fellow—difference in dress (slick fellow dresses flashily, looks like a neon sign; quiet fellow always looks and feels a little awkward in a suit of any kind, is more the sports clothes, casual type), difference in manner of speech (slick fellow talks rapidly, slangily, steadily; quiet fellow chooses his words and doesn't say much), difference in social skill (slick fellow is expert dancer; quiet fellow is awkward on dance floor), and so on—you've done a thorough job of characterization on both of them.

In other words, the success of your characterizations depends upon the ease with which your readers can distinguish between your story people and recognize their separate personalities. Whether you give them extreme characteristics (for example, one cowardly and one very brave), or whether you make them similar in type but opposite in manner, the important thing is that you make them distinguishable from one another.

You begin to characterize the moment you form the broad outlines of your plot, because you are assigning your characters to roles which will require different actions, reactions, and motivations from each of them. These basic assignments are your kickoff in the job of characterization; the characters' reasons for wanting to solve the problem or (in the case of the opposition) for keeping it from being solved, and their general moves to achieve their purpose, will begin to show generally what kind of people they are. But don't stop there: the characterizations will be full-grown only if you follow them through into all the specific details of the story as well.

It is possible, for example, for you to have a character act with logical motivation and right in line with his "side" in the story—that is, heroically or villainously, sympathetically or unsympathetically—and still miss a first-grade opportunity for some more characterization.

Let us say, for example, that you want to characterize a villain as generally sneaky and underhanded in his tactics; yet you run a scene in which the hero goes to an auction to bid on a house he needs desperately, and the villain outbids him and gets the house. The villain's actions are perfectly logical, and properly dastardly, but there's nothing sneaky or underhanded about them. You'd have added another milestone in your job of characterizing the villain as sneaky and underhanded if he had gotten the house in a crooked manner—perhaps by bribing the auctioneer to "overlook" the hero's upraised hand.

It is not a requirement for a story person to reveal his characterized qualities in every action he makes. We've already discussed the error of making your characters unbelievably all-black or all-white, and it will usually do the trick if the villain is shown as more often villainous than good, and the hero as more often good than bad. On the other hand, characterization becomes more pronounced through continued showing of a specific quality or type of action, and good opportunities to show it are sometimes hard to come by. If one presents itself, it is best to grab it and make full use of it.

I have mentioned one of the opportunities for characterization in different types of clothing; there are many others. A girl who wears too much make-up, no brassière, and a dress which is several sizes too tight and features an extremely low-cut neckline, is characterized almost immediately; though there may be exceptions to the rule, it is doubtful that her favorite sport is singing at church socials. A girl with no make-up, thick glasses, and an unfashionable hairdo is characterized in the other direction. Use this sort of thing when you can.

You'll also help differentiate between your characters by

differentiating between their physical descriptions in general. Try to avoid having two fat little men in the same story, or two thin young fellows with horn-rimmed glasses, or two dark-haired young ladies with pixie haircuts, or two men with hairline mustaches.

The same, of course, applies to your choice of names for your characters. If you have a character named Robertson, don't call another one Williamson. Avoid Jack and Jake, and Larry and Harry. That should be the case even with twins, unless they almost always appear together in the story and their separate actions have no importance. In general, try to avoid two names which sound alike, begin or end alike or similarly, or begin with the same initial.

The character tag is another device which is pretty much dead today because of overuse. This is the stunt wherein a story person is characterized and recognized by his constant repetition of the same act, such as flipping a half dollar into the air, or the same phrase or type of phrase, such as, "Bless my topknot!" It is still possible, I suppose, to think up a fresh character tag, and restrain yourself from using it so often in the story that it becomes irritating as well as characterizing; but you'd be much better off skipping this trick entirely. Except in stories about long-established series characters, where the public has learned to sigh and take it, most editors react to character tags today by murmuring, "Bless my topknot!" flipping a rejection slip into the air, and then attaching it to the manuscript.

27

AND THEY LIVED HAPPILY EVER AFTER:
The ending

Just as there are three points at which a story can be opened, there are also three points at which it can be closed. These points are just before the solution is reached, just as the solution is reached, and just after the solution is reached.

Here is an example of the just-before-the-solution ending:

He was sure now, and his footsteps quickened as the house came into sight. It had never been Linda, never at all; it had always been Mary. What a damned fool a man can make of himself!

Maybe it was too late now . . . but at least there was hope. Mary had always understood him, even when he had been too thickheaded or stubborn to understand himself. Maybe she would understand that this was just another of his damnfool stunts, though by far the biggest one. At least, he knew, it would be his last.

The house looked just the same, and the sight of it up close was a wonderful thing. He squared his shoulders a little, and put his key in the door.

In the strictest sense, the just-before ending doesn't really happen just before the solution: it happens just before the *full* solution. As in the example given, which is a closing excerpt from a decision-between-wife-and-young-girl story, the main problem is usually resolved, but the question of whether or not the lead character will achieve full happiness is left unanswered, with only hope shown. In this story, the lead character has solved his problem because he has made the correct choice between his girl friend, Linda, and his wife, Mary, but the full solution is not shown because it is not absolutely certain as the story closes whether or not Mary will take him back.

The just-before ending, of course, occurs in the unresolved story. It is a perfectly acceptable way to conclude a story when the nature of the story events seems to demand that sort of ending, but it might be a good idea to keep in mind, as I have indicated, that "unresolved" is usually a misnomer, and not-fully-resolved is really meant. The reader will feel cheated after the big problem build-up, if, at the conclusion, a solution is not at least hinted or promised: even if the solution is only— as in the You Can't Win stories—the fact that the problem is unbeatable.

In the example given, no full solution is shown because that is as it should be. Despite the reader's sympathy for the lead character, he knows that the lead has come very close to making an immensely serious blunder, and he doesn't *want* the lead to be forgiven too quickly or easily. He is pretty sure, however, from the indications in the final paragraphs, that Mary *will eventually* take the lead character back, and so he is satisfied.

Here is an example of the just-as-the-solution ending:

McCoy nodded to the police officers. "All right," he said, "he's admitted it. You'd better take him away. I'll see you down at the Hall later on."

He turned and smiled at Ellen. "You'd better give me a couple of dozen kisses right now," he said. "I'm going to be pretty busy in my first few weeks as the new district attorney."

The just-as ending gives the solution in all its details, and then cuts right off. It does so smoothly, of course, with a little concluding sentence or paragraph such as the one in this example, but the solution scene is always the last one.

And here is an example of the just-after-the-solution ending. It comes from a story in which a sort of running gag has been made of the father's frequent bawlings-out of his son for leaving roller skates on the floor. Later on, however, the son is seriously injured in a school fire, and this is the way the story ends:

Joe replaced the telephone on its stand, and looked at his wife. Her eyes were wide and frightened, and he took both of her hands gently in his.

"It's all right, Alice," he said. "It's all right. The Doc says I got him to the hospital in time. He says Lonny will be out of there and all fixed up in just a few weeks. . . ."

His grip tightened on his wife's hands. "It's fixed me up, too, Alice," he said. "You'll never have to worry about my running away from trouble again."

They stood there in silence for a moment, and then Joe grinned and let her go. "Hey," he said, "I've got to tell Rod! He's probably sitting there in his house and chewing his fingernails to pieces. I won't phone him—I think I'll run over there so I can watch his face when I tell him."

He kissed her, and hurried out of the room and along the corridor to the stairs. He had just reached the stairs when his foot caught in a roller skate on the floor, and he slid to the edge of the top stair and past. He didn't quite manage to grab the railing.

He thumped and bumped down the stairs, and, the roller skate still clinging to his shoe, began to slide again—along the bottom floor and out the open door and down the outer stairs. He hit the sidewalk with a thud which shook the nearby trees.

He sat there, stunned, for a little while, and then got gingerly to his feet and rubbed himself. He stooped and picked up the roller skate, opened his mouth to cuss, and then grinned instead. When he looked up again, his next-door neighbor was standing nearby and staring at him.

He returned the stare. "Well, what do you want?" he asked belligerently. "What's wrong with leaving roller skates on the floor? How else can a guy get any exercise around this place?"

The final scene in the just-after ending is, of course, an anti-climax. The important action actually ends when Joe tells his wife that Lonny is okay, and also reveals that *he* is now going to be okay (for the problem of the story is his weakness of character and habit of always running away from trouble instead of facing it squarely). The roller-skate scene is not vital to the plot by any means.

Generally, anticlimaxes are bad stuff. The reader is built up all through the story to wait for the solution, and, therefore, once that solution arrives, he is satisfied and all through with the story—and any action which follows the solution scene is just so much excess baggage, and uninteresting to him. The story has climbed to the top of the hill with the solution scene, and anticlimactic action thereafter just begins to roll it down the other side.

The just-after ending, however, makes the anticlimactic scene satisfactory because it is a very short anticlimax, and because it has had so much heralding throughout the story (in this case, all the earlier fuss about the skates) that it becomes a sort of extra fillip—icing on the cake rather than excess baggage. The roller-skate scene is not uninteresting; it is very brief, and, in addition to bringing the running gag to an amusing conclusion, it integrates very well with the solution scene because it is, when you get right down to it, just further and heart-warming proof of the father's relief over his son's salvation and his own.

Avoid anticlimaxes which have not been given earlier heralding in the story, which are not the fitting conclusion to earlier plants. And avoid *any* anticlimaxes which are too long: which run into a long scene or several scenes after the solution has been reached, or which relate the characters' histories too far into the future. (The fairy-tale or down-through-the-third-generation anticlimax fits into the to-be-avoided category: *And they always lived happily after that, and had fine children, and, later on, fine grandchildren.* The reader is interested in the solution of the *lead character's* problem, not in his subsequent career as a grandparent.)

If you have a sufficiently strong problem and solution, long anticlimactic details are usually unnecessary, because the solution will generally tell the reader all he has to know—and he can imagine or predict the lead's future from the solution. If long explanations are necessary, it is best to get them right into the solution scene before the final and closing piece of important action; in a detective story, for example, all the details which led to the discovery of the killer should be related *before* the killer jumps on the hero and is beaten down and led away by the gendarmes. But if you have planted a running gag which leads right to an inevitable fillip or icing-on-the-cake, and can keep that anticlimactic scene very short, it will do no harm.

It does not, incidentally, always have to be a running gag in the humorous sense; it can also be a sequence of serious little events which lead to a satisfying finish. For example, a cowardly lead character can always get pushed around by a big tough guy, and then, after he has licked his cowardice in some other way in the solution scene, go back and beat hell out of the tough guy.

Use the just-before ending in stories where the full solution will obviously take a long time and a lot of slow mending—such as the example given. Use the just-as ending when the solution ties up everything extremely satisfactorily and an extra fillip is neither desired nor needed. And use the just-after ending in those cases as discussed.

The punch-line ending has received a great deal of attention and publicity. It is the opposite-pole brother of the narrative hook: just as the narrative hook in its basic form tries to pull the reader into the story with an outstanding first sentence, the punch line tries to send him off smiling happily or dreamily or feeling otherwise satisfied with an outstanding last sentence.

An excellent example of the punch line at its best occurs in the stage version of *Arsenic and Old Lace*. In this play, for those who have not seen or read it, the hero is bedeviled by the fact that all the other members of his family are homicidally insane, and, as a result, works hard to avoid the heroine because she has marital ideas. At the end, however, he learns that he is not a member of the family at all, but actually the illegitimate son of a servant, and he rushes up to the heroine and takes her in his arms.

"Darling," he shouts ecstatically. "I'm a *bastard!*"

Like the narrative hook, the punch line has been so much overused that good examples today are extremely rare. If you think of it, therefore, only as the very last line of your story, you may easily go awry. Just try to make the entire concluding section of your story satisfying and pleasing to your reader, and you'll do fine.

FOUR: THE FINISHED-
PRODUCT FACTS

28

THE SLICE AND THE SLASH: *Revision*

The best way to feel about revision is that you want to do as little as possible of it in the course of your part- or full-time writing career.

Some writers believe that the only way to create a first-grade, salable story is to write it and then revise it very extensively, cutting and altering and rewriting words, phrases, sentences, paragraphs, and even entire scenes. Their idea is that a story must be polished, repolished, and then polished some more in order to make it fully right. It is a common enough theory, but I think that most writers who actually do create first-grade, salable stories regularly will agree that it is a fallacious one.

I have already mentioned the primary danger in planning to do extensive revisions on your stories: the fact that the subconscious realization that there *will* be further revisions tends to create carelessness in the writing of the first draft (less and less care in the choice of language and phrasing, less and less effort for clarity and the right dramatic effect the first time), with the end result that the first drafts become worse and worse, and the revisions heavier and heavier, until the author has almost lost altogether his ability to write clearly and well. You become too dependent, in other words, on the loophole of "fixing it up later."

There are, of course, other dangers. Another lies in the fact that, however callous you may become about story writing as you remain in the writing business, or however new you may be at the game now, you will still write your first draft most of the time "in emotional heat." In other words, however rapidly you pound out your stories or however ploddingly you set down phrase after phrase, you will still feel the emotional impact of the story events when you first write them, and will pass on that feeling most freshly and vividly in the first draft. When, however, you do many subsequent drafts, you are no longer writing emotionally and freshly; you are going over the same stuff again and again and again and doing the routine job of fixing and patching up. You may improve the wording here and there, and substitute better-phrased paragraphs and sections here and there, but, because the emotional drive is gone and you're working and thinking routinely, you will often polish out the freshness and emotional tone at the same time.

Furthermore, there is a saturation point in excessive revision which is not too hard to reach. As you continue to revise and revise and go over the same ground again and again, you'll eventually become so familiar with the exact phrasing and movement of the story that you'll lose your perspective: you'll become so close to the story and so imbued with it that you'll no longer be able to tell accurately which things are right and which are not so good. And it is a sad thing to contemplate the death blow you can deal a story when you have reached that point but still think you're revising intelligently.

Another objection to excessive revision, particularly since it so often does more harm than good, is that it takes so much time away from *new* work—you're patching up and patching up (and possibly ruining) one story, when you could be spending the time writing others and thus smoothing out your style and getting yourself better represented with manuscripts at the markets. And one last objection is that, as you become an established professional, circumstances may arise where you won't be able to do heavy revising—for example, where you're given an excellent and high-paying story assignment with a very short deadline, or where you're given adequate time before deadline but things like family troubles prevent you from working until almost the last moment. If you're physically and mentally unable to turn out a first or second draft which is right, you're sunk.

In general, the best practice is the one indicated at the start of this chapter: try to revise as little as possible by revising only when absolutely necessary. If you can't manage a white paper first-and-final draft, go ahead and do your first draft on yellow paper—but train yourself to write so tightly and carefully that only a limited number of minor revisions are usually necessary before you can retype and get the story to market. When you finish your draft, it is certainly wise to go over it with a blue pencil and an eagle eye, but make changes only where they are definitely and indisputably necessary—where a word or phrase or section is positively wrong in meaning, or where a word or phrase or section positively does not give the dramatic effect it must give, or something of that sort. Be honest with yourself and, when you're about to alter something for no stronger reason than a whim, or make a substitution which really isn't a heck of a lot better than the original, leave the story alone.

Your initial choice of words and material, made during the emotional drive of creation and in context with the surrounding sentences and the mood of the story, will usually be best, anyhow. You'll find that, as you develop the habit of tight writing and revision only where really necessary, your stories will grow better and the sections which require revision will show up less and less often.

You will probably hear, now and then, of the "cooler" or icebox method of revision—wherein the writer puts a script away in a drawer the moment he has completed the initial draft, and takes it out and revises it a month or two later, when he has cooled off about the story and can be completely objective in his examination. I have known a great many authors who have tried the icebox system, but know almost none who have found it to be of any real value, or whose stories have been done more good than harm by it. The trouble with the method is that, just as too constant association with a story during revision after revision puts the writer too close to it to see and feel it clearly, too long dissociation puts the writer too far away from it to see and feel it clearly. The author can never become *entirely* objective about his story—as, for example, an editor seeing it for the first time would be—because he still retains memories of the processes of writing it and of the emotional mood at that time; but if he is put far enough away from the story and out of its mood, as occurs due to the passage of time while the story's in the icebox, it is difficult to get "inside" the story again and *feel* where the dramatic effects are inadequate, and the like, when he returns to it once more after the cooling-off period.

It is best, all in all, to attack your necessary revisions when you've just finished your first draft and still retain some of the heat and emotional drive of creation: and, by doing so, also get the story completely off your work schedule and your mind so you can be ready for your next job.

Sometimes, of course, you will pronounce a story completely okay just as it comes out of the typewriter or after you've made some revisions, and send it off to market—and then learn that some additional revision work is necessary. This occurs when an editor spots or thinks he spots a flaw or a place for improvement in your story, and indicates that he will buy it if necessary repairs are made.

Let's have a look at when to do the revision, and how.

First of all, *don't* rush to your blue pencil and typewriter and begin to revise a story just because an editor has returned it with a comment such as "too slight" or "too little fast action." A comment of that sort usually means that the editor thought your story considerably above the average of those he rejected that day, and that he felt it showed promise and he would like to see others from you, but it is by no means a commitment or even an indication that he will buy the story if you eliminate or improve the factor about which he has commented.

You must remember that the editor is not in his job to serve as a one-man criticism bureau. He knows there is something basically wrong with your story which makes it necessary that he reject rather than purchase it, and he jots down the quick comment to guide you on future stories and to express his interest, but he generally has neither the time nor the inclination to give you a full analysis. The point about which he has commented may not even be the thing which is really wrong with the story, because an experienced editor knows a yarn is off the beam, often without quite knowing why, the moment he reads it, and his comment is a quick guess as to the reason; but a careful, thought-out-at-length analysis on his part might reveal that the reason was something else again. Or, it may not be the full objection, or it may only be the strongest of a number of objections.

In most cases, you'll only irritate the editor when you interpret his friendly comment as a suggestion for revision and alter the story and send it back to him. Your best bet, when you get a comment of that sort, is to note it as an expression of interest, and write a new story which seems to cover the objection and send it to the editor promptly. No covering letter is necessary; he'll recognize your by-line if he's interested in you.

A critical comment from an editor is not necessarily a sign to revise the story and fix that point to make it right for other markets, either. Much of the time, the editor's comment will refer only to his own market. The story which he criticizes as having too little fast action, for example, will often he just right for the next market on the list, whose editor doesn't like quite as much action. When, of course, a number of editors make the same comment, it is time to take the story off in a corner and see what all the objecting is about.

It is another matter again, naturally, when an editor writes you a detailed letter stating that he likes your story very much, but is returning it because of some specific objection. If you can think of a way to rewrite the story and eliminate the objection in a manner which will be logical and won't otherwise injure the yarn and make it unacceptable for another reason, you should certainly do so and make the sale. But first write the editor, thank him for his letter, and outline your idea and ask him if he believes the story will be acceptable if you eliminate the objection in that way. If he says, "Yes," or "Probably," get to work.

Most of the time, however, an editor who wants a rewrite will return your story together with a specific request that you do one (or write you and ask that you work from your carbon and send him revised versions of pages Such-and-Such), and he'll give you general details on how he wants you to go about it. That usually won't constitute a definite commitment, either, because few editors will make a commitment on an imperfect story unless they know your stuff and are sure that you can make it perfect, but you'll almost always get a purchase check if you fix up the point as requested. When you begin your revision, you won't have much trouble getting back "into" the story, as in the icebox situation, however cold the yarn may have grown: because there's no problem here of puzzling out which things to revise, and how to do so. Just follow the editor's directions closely.

Don't, by the way, become revision happy in the process, and change six or seven other things while you're fixing the one the editor has requested. You may alter or eliminate the very things the editor likes about your story. And if the revision is a fairly extensive one, don't just cross out words and lines and write or type over them. Retype all the revised pages.

Once in a great while, an editor will make a request for a revision, and you'll look over the story and see that he has missed a point and that the revision is actually unnecessary. He will, for example, say that it is never explained how the hero escaped from the ropes which bind him while he is a captive in the old deserted factory owned by the villain, and yet, on page 19, you have a paragraph which tells how the hero tips over a jar of acid and burns off the ropes and gets loose.

When that sort of thing happens, you will know, more than ever before in your life, the sensation of an irresistible urge. The desire to write the editor and laugh at him about it will be so strong that you may have to lock yourself up in a closet for a few hours until you get over it. If necessary, lock yourself in the closet—but don't, whatever you do, write him and laugh at him about it.

He can have two answers to your letter. If he's in a good mood, or if he's a good guy, he will reply and point out that, if he missed it, so may a great many of his magazine's readers, and you'd better go into more detail in that scene and make it more visible; or he may laugh at his oversight, too, and ask you to return the script intact so that he can buy it. If he isn't, he may also do either of these two things, but thereafter he may easily manage to get along without more of your stuff.

So, if you see that the editor has missed the point, just go ahead—without bothering him—and build it up in greater detail and make it more visible. When you get your check, you may, if you like, chuckle quietly to yourself as you cash it and spend the money.

29

MARKETING AND AGENTS: *Where to go*
with the completed story

When you have finished plotting and writing and revising
your stories, you will want to know how to go about selling
them. There are, of course, two methods: submitting them
directly to the publishing houses, or submitting them to the
publishing houses through a reliable literary agent.

Let's have a look, first of all, at the literary-agent situation.
I covered the subject of literary agencies pretty thoroughly
in an article called "Can We Still Be Friends?" which was
published in the trade journal, *Writer's Digest*, and quote
largely from this article in the material on agents which follows:

A few feet from my desk, off in a dark corner, there's a curious
spot on the wall which looks scarred and lacerated and about to
cave in. As a matter of fact, it *is* about to cave in—for it has
received harsh treatment through the years. It is the section
of the wall against which I beat my head.

Most of my clients and potential clients, I'm happy to report,
are awfully nice. We exchange lovingly cordial letters when I
get them better rates than they expected, and icily cordial ones
when I have to confess that I argued for more money with
an editor for two hours and he won—and when they come to
New York, sometimes I buy them Scotch or Pink Ladies, and
sometimes they buy Cuba Libres for me.

Sometimes, however, some of their requests and questions can, as I say, send an agent, sobbing bitterly, out of his chair to see which is harder—his head or the wall. I'd like to discuss and attempt to clarify some of the more recurrent insanity in-spirers, and in that way, perhaps, straighten out some points in the minds of those of you who are contemplating getting agents but don't quite understand their operating methods.

Here, then, are the letters which earn cold glances:

1. The enclosed story has been rejected by a total of forty-seven magazines. I know, however, that you agents have influence with editors and publishers, so please sell it for me as soon as possible.

There isn't an agent in the business who has ever sold a bad story, article, or book because of personal friendship or influ-ence with an editor or publisher. Most agents have no objection to seeing heavily rejected scripts because they feel they may do a better job of market selection than the author has done, and not because they hope that influence will turn the trick even if the story is a poor one. If that was your reason for thinking of signing up with an agent, you'd better forget about it.

The only reason an agent is able to sell a story is that the story is a good and salable story. No agent is better than the clients he represents—and no agent has ever been able to sell a poor story because he happens to be an agent. With similar stories of equal value, sometimes, editorial friendship will tip the scales.

But if an editor begins to buy poor stuff from an agent friend, the overpowering odor of the material will soon come to the publisher's attention—and the editor will go out on his ear. What, then, was the point in the carefully cultivated friendship some writers think agents spend their time building? And if the agent's friendship is with the publisher himself, even the publisher can't buy sickening yarns—or the reading public will give him hell and turn to a rival publication whose publisher doesn't have an unscrupulous agent friend.

An agent, generally speaking, has three values as far as the writer is concerned: (1) If he's honest and on the level, he can furnish you with frank evaluations of your stuff, tell you truthfully and expertly about your weak points and strong points—something your family and friends will not or cannot do. (2) He spends every working day in the publishing area—visiting editors, talking to editors on the phone, lunching with editors, sometimes lugging his wife over for games of bridge with editors and their wives. Because of this, he knows the day-by-day things which go on in the field—which magazines are buying heavily and which are temporarily stocked, particular tastes and taboos and eccentricities and buying habits of editors, those special and sudden needs which mean assignments—and he can bring you heavier sales of your material, perhaps sales to better markets than the ones for which you planned your yarns, and up-to-the-minute trend tips. (3) Equally important, he is a third person. If you write an editor and tell him how superb your story really is, or how much you deserve a raise in rates, you sound conceited and may antagonize him—even if your story *is* good, or if you *do* deserve a raise. But an agent may do this because he's not talking about his own work: if he is enthusiastic about a story or asks for more money, it's all right.

2. I don't want an agent who acts as a messenger service. Please inform me by return special delivery air mail whether or not you submit in person everything you handle.

Of course I don't—and it's about time that fond illusion is dispelled. No agent submits in person all the material he handles.

If his morning mail turns up a story which he thinks is the best he has ever read and which he feels will become an age-less classic, there's no question in the world but that he'll telephone an editor and howl ecstatically about it, or make an appointment with an editor and go over and plug the yarn to the skies. If a salable article comes in, he'll surely telephone a few editors to determine their attitude toward the subject before sending it along. Or if a script of the length and type an editor has requested comes along, or a script by a writer in whom the agent has interested an editor, of course the agent will phone and say, "Joe, I'm sending you a new yarn by Mc-Foop," or, "Bill, I've got an appointment near your office. I'll stop by and give you a first-rate novelette which has just come in."

But as far as the usual case is concerned—well, most agents employ messengers, and a few employ the same government men in gray you use when you send your material directly to magazines. If a script rates special attention or heralding of some kind, you may be sure it will get it, through an attached note, a phone call, or a personal visit—but when the script is a typical good script, just right for an editor and exactly like three or four others in that respect, there's nothing to be accomplished by personal delivery.

The value of an agent's "messenger service," of course, is that it is his business to know exactly where the script must go. The unagented writer may send a novelette to a magazine whose inventory is loaded with novelettes, or an article to a magazine which has just bought or run a similar article, but the good agent, who—himself and through his staff—reads all major magazines and keeps up to the second on market information, will almost never do this. He'll know that another magazine is *light* on novelettes, and he'll know another magazine likely to snap up an article on your subject, and you'll have a sale instead of a perhaps unexplained rejection.

3. Tell me, do you think it's true that agents who charge fees are off the level? My cousin works in a bar, and a writer who used to come in there and cadge drinks told him that a good agent doesn't charge fees.

No, kiddo, I don't think it's true. You see, *we* charge fees our-selves for reading, analyzing, and making detailed reports on stories by unestablished writers.

During the earlier days of my agency, we charged no fees for one simple reason: we accepted only established writers with established reputations. There was no reason under the sun to charge fees to examine and report on incoming stuff: our clients had sold enough to justify the conclusion that their output was almost always salable as it stood, and we knew we'd derive our profit from the commission on sales. We knew, too, that the commissions would be regular enough to cover all overhead and pay off the butcher and baker as well.

Many agencies work that way today. They handle the top names only and won't handle you until you become a top name yourself, and they don't charge fees because, when you're added to their list, your stuff is so professional and your sales chances always so good that it isn't necessary. They've got an important and urgent place in the field—they take business worries off the hands of busy professionals.

I decided to add promising new writers, and writers for lesser fields than the slicks, to our agency list because, in the course of an expansion program some years ago, I hired several additional staff members who were fresh and bright and full of good ideas. An agency built of household-name clients is a fine thing, they pointed out, but to add only writers who have already arrived is a halfway measure. There are many fine writers who never arrive because of poor market sense or because nobody ever gets around to straightening out the tech-nical flaws in their stuff—and if newer writers could be sifted through and the promising people *groomed* for major sales, it would easily be worth while. This was in line with my own thinking, and I agreed, provided overhead would be covered while the grooming is going on.

That phrase—"provided overhead be covered"—is the answer to fees, and the reason so many agents charge them. Newer writers may believe they know technique backward and forward, but in many cases it turns out that they've misunderstood or misinterpreted the rules and their stuff is full of holes. These errors must be corrected: the agent and his staff must write long letters of advice and analysis, pushing the newcomer's stuff into proper channels, until he straightens out and begins to sell. And even these beginning sales mean nothing, for until the sales become steady and regular, the agent's time spent in the selling eats up the profit.

During this period, the agent must be paid for the time spent away from his arrived clients—his staff must be paid, his electricity and stationery and telephone bills must be covered. Most agents, you will find, charge fees so low that they obviously only cover overhead—and proof of the pudding is in the fact that all agents drop fees after they make several sales for a client.

Our decision to handle new writers as well as established people, incidentally, was one of the happiest moves we've ever made, since so very many of the top writers on our list today first came to us in that way: with no sales at all to their credit. And that, of course, is the reason we now have an absolute policy of pushing a new writer's script as hard as scripts by our biggest names: we know through happy experience that the new writer, whose scripts today bring in small commissions, may well be the man or woman writing the hot, big-money properties tomorrow.

The average agency fee runs around one dollar per thousand words of manuscript, with a minimum fee of five dollars for scripts under five thousand words, and flat rates for very long manuscripts such as books (generally twenty-five dollars for scripts up to 150,000 words, fifty dollars for scripts above that length). This usually includes all service—reading, detailed analysis and report, assistance and advice for necessary revisions, marketing, etc. The only additional charge is the commission upon sale of the manuscript, which is the same as that charged on scripts by established writers: 10 per cent on sales made to United States markets, and 15 to 20 per cent on sales to Canadian, British, and other foreign markets (because the agent must maintain a separate office or affiliates in the foreign countries).

4. I understand that you handle on straight commission basis writers who have been selling regularly. I've sold $620 worth of news reporting to *Feed Grinder*, and now I want to write humorous fiction for the slicks. I presume you'll handle me on straight commission basis and without fee charges. What do you say?

Usually I say "No," for this fellow doesn't really understand the purpose of fees, and probably suspects agents invented them just to annoy him personally.

We charge a fee in the first place because we want our basic expenses to be covered while we're working with a writer who hasn't proven himself through steady sales—and we skip fees with a writer who has been selling regularly to good national markets because we feel that he's proven himself sufficiently professional to take the chance of working with him without coverage of overhead and profit prior to commission on sales. But the point is that, if we're not going to charge him coverage-of-overhead fees, he must have a sales record which will justify it.

The facts that a writer has achieved considerable success in trade news reporting doesn't give any clue at all to his abilities as a writer of fiction in the light vein. He may be a dud or he may be a master: but, if he should turn out to be a dud, we can't afford to analyze his stuff and work him into the slicks without charge simply because he's a great success in a totally different field.

If a successful pulp writer wants to try to break into the slicks, for example, I'm always happy to take him on, on commission—because pulp fiction is in its elements much like all other commercial fiction, and the two are close enough. If a slick magazine article writer wants us to handle his occasional attempts at romantic verse, that's all right—and we'll be happy to do it, for the article sales commissions cover the additional expense of selling verse at seven dollars and fifty cents a throw, and the author's soul is at peace.

But if you've had some success in one field and want to go into an entirely different one, don't expect an agent to work his head off breaking you into the new field without payment of fees.

5. Hiss, hiss. You returned my story, "He Done Killed Her Dead," with a letter explaining why it was unsalable. You'll be amazed to hear that *Independent Corn-Pone Grower* has just bought it, and scheduled it for their Fall-Winter issue.

My reaction to this sort of thing is generally, Great going, pal, and many more—but the *Independent Corn-Pone Grower* only pays five bucks for material.

Although some writers do not realize it, it must be understood by you that a literary agency is not entirely a benevolent association—but is engaged in making money so that the owner and his staff keep off Skid Row. And the commission on a five-dollar sale, I can tell you without pausing to count on my fingers, is only fifty cents—not even enough these days to buy permission to step into a restaurant and sniff deeply.

Occasionally an agent will make a sale to a very minor magazine because the script won't go in any of the better ones, and the writer is either a newcomer who can use the emotional stimulus of a sale, or an old-timer who can use money in any shape, form, or amount. But there is a limit to these things: obviously, when an agent has exhausted all the best markets and all the fair ones, he simply cannot afford to continue with the tiny ones—and occasionally a script sells to these tiny ones, the markets to which the agent cannot afford to submit.

Have the same consideration for the agent he tries to have for you. Don't ask him to handle your output if you plan to specialize in fillers, or religious-market material, which sells for a few dollars apiece. And don't expect him to continue trying a yarn right down to the experimental journals which pay their writers with subscriptions. An agent who tries to pay his rent with 10 per cent of subscriptions will quickly find himself outside his office building.

Another answer to the fact that writers sometimes sell work returned by agents is that de Lawd never quite got around to making any of us perfect. A very good agent I know received a story from a client who was a comparatively new writer, and didn't like it too much, but he sent it to a magazine anyhow because the editors there were especially receptive to newcomers. When the magazine returned it with a cold comment, he decided his original opinion had been backed up, and returned the story to its author. The author sent it off to another top slick which promptly bought it.

When you consider, however, that this was the agent's second major error in judgment in nearly fourteen years, you've got to admit that the record isn't a bad one.

6. Please send me eleven bank references, your certificate of citizenship, and a sworn statement testifying that you have been vaccinated against inflamed gums. I was recently gypped like all get-out by an agent whose office was four blocks from your own, and I'm afraid that you may be a dangerous criminal, too.

The answer to that one is that there have been thieves and incompetents in every industry and profession from bootblacking to banking to bazooka-making to the Presidency of the United States—and it seems somewhat wildly imaginative to assume that a black hood should be placed over an entire field because one member is a bad un. Jack the Ripper was possibly also an editor, as a disgruntled writer once assured me, but there are still some awfully nice guys among editors.

Generally speaking, an agent who has many established professionals among his clients is bound to be honest and reliable—because writers pass the word around quickly when an agent is shady, and the shady agent's list quickly dissolves or never gets built up. There's one way to find out about an agent's clients, incidentally: write and ask him.

Occasionally, of course, an agent who has worked honorably for writers for years will suddenly go screwball and pull all kinds of stunts, as was the case with one some years ago. This is the sort of thing that no one can predict—and is perhaps caused by temporary or permanent insanity, glandular trouble, or an overdose of Serutan. It is in the class with bank tellers who are honest for twenty years and suddenly rush off with a satchelful of money and is a chance you must take— like the chance you take when you turn in a suit or dress to the dry cleaner's. He may be gone, clothing and all, the next morning: but if he's been in business for a while and has a reputation for honesty, the chances are that he won't.

7. I sent you a story on Monday, and here it is Thursday and I haven't heard from you. What's the matter—you lose my script or something?

No, we haven't, friend. We're still working on it, so hold your horses.

Most agencies begin work on material almost immediately after its arrival. After the script has been carded and otherwise registered, it is turned over to the agency head or his staff for reading, and if immediately salable is sent out to market.

Sometimes, however, it isn't. It displays certain important flaws, yet at the same time it displays a lot of good writing and some evident ability. That makes it a problem—it isn't quite right for offer for sale, it can't be returned for a rewrite because the fault is in the basic framework itself and that would amount to writing an entirely new story, and yet it isn't bad enough to be returned with suggestion to destroy. There's a staff meeting called: sometimes, when the script is really a puzzler, two or three meetings. All this takes time: for, though the script may be enough of a hair-grayer to interest everybody, discussions and meetings on it must be sandwiched between work on other pressing matters. The average agency report is sent within two weeks, and many times (as in the case with established professionals, whose scripts can usually go out for sale immediately) even by return mail, but you must realize that work is being performed for your own good even if a month passes without report.

And if a script is okayed and sent to market, the agent cannot send the writer a play-by-play description of what is happening to it, though he will, of course, inform the writer initially that it has gone out for sale. The agent reports to the author whenever he has news, a sale, a requested rewrite from an editor, an important editorial comment, or something of that sort. He just cannot, however, inform the author each time a script has not made the grade at a market and gone to another, or he would have no time to do anything else.

Generally, for the reason of the rush-and-unrush piles system, plus the fact that agents who consistently send good material to editors will naturally get prompter attention, literary agents get fast reports on material they send to market. Sometimes, however, editors get bogged down with other work and take longer in their reporting; in those cases, the agent's only choice is to prod them gently as much as possible but mostly grin and bear it. And then, of course, the agent's own report to you of eventual sale will be slower in coming.

Just remember that the key to happiness lies in that adage laid down long, long ago: if you want to stay sane, forget about a script the moment it leaves your home, and concentrate on new material.

If you decide to submit directly to publishing houses instead of working though an agent, there are two things you must do to familiarize yourself with market needs and otherwise keep in touch with your business. First, as I have told you, read the magazines to which you submit, and read them regularly and carefully. And second, read the writers' trade journals.

The authorship journals are to writers what medical journals are to doctors: they serve as clearing houses for information on new techniques, new angles on old techniques, and all other technique information of value to the worker in the field. In addition, these publications report important events in the publishing world such as short-story prize contests and the birth of new magazines, and from time to time publish full lists of markets and needs. Writers' magazines may be secured at larger newsstands or at your public library, and you'll find them stimulating and helpful reading whether or not you work through an agent.

When you get your specific choice of markets down pat, there are several things to keep in mind about the marketing itself.

Try to keep yourself, first of all, from becoming discouraged and giving up on a story because it piles up a few rejections. Some stories hit the right market at the right time and sell at first submission, or within two or three submissions; other stories, just as good, may run into overstocks and other situations and may take a lot of offering around before they sell. Almost everyone who has been in the writing business for some time can think of dozens of cases of manuscripts which had been rejected at market after market and then finally sold for high prices. Only recently, for example, my agency took on a story which was an odd sort of job and which we knew would be hard to sell, but which we liked very much, and we offered it to forty markets without acceptance or even encouragement. The forty-first market bought it gladly, paid a top price for it, and subsequently an outstanding book publisher saw the story in print and was so impressed with it that negotiations have begun for the author to do a novel for his firm.

If you have real faith in a story, keep it going to market after market until every logical possibility has been exhausted. Retype it every once in a while if it looks soiled or wrinkled, and then get it off in the mails again.

The second point is that it is perfectly acceptable to submit a story to more than one magazine published by the same chain or company, provided that each magazine has a different editor or editorial director. If your writer's magazine market guides show that two magazines are managed by the same editor, or that an entire group of magazines is under the editorial direction of one man, there is no point in submitting to each of them because the same editor and staff read all submissions as possibilities for each of the magazines—and rejection means that they don't feel it is right for any. When, however, your guides show that several magazines are published by one company but each is under different editorship, you may consider them as though they were entirely apart, and submit your story, provided it fits the markets, to each one in turn.

I might add, of course, that it is considered unethical to submit a story to more than one market at a time, because of the irritations and mix-ups which might occur if you sent out several copies of the same story and several different editors bought the story simultaneously: and it is regarded as unwise to send an editor several of your stories at once, because he may tend to consider them collectively instead of giving each one individual attention. Nor is it wise to inform an editor that a story has previously been seen and rejected by other magazines: however fair-minded he may be, and however much he may feel that he wants what he wants and doesn't care whether or not others wanted it, he may still form an unconscious prejudice against it.

Make sure, too, that you keep careful records of the markets to which you have submitted each story: you don't want to forget and return a story to an editor who has already seen and rejected it. The only time it is really safe to resubmit a story to a market which has already seen it is when you read in a writers' magazine that there has been a reorganization at the market and the staff entirely changed.

30

JUST SIGN HERE, PLEASE: *Contracts, rights, and other legal matters*

The usual contract between author and publisher for the purchase of magazine material is a little notice which is typed or printed on the reverse side of the payment check. It is far less formidable in appearance than the usual book contract, which is a separate document and may run as long as five or six pages of fine print, but it is not one bit less binding or important.

Sometimes the magazine contract runs only about six words in length, aside from the title of your story; all it says is, "For all rights to work entitled . . ." You cannot, of course, alter this notice in any way, because that will invalidate the check and the deal. And when you endorse the check and deposit it to your account or otherwise cash it, you have sold the publisher full ownership of that story: the right to publish it in his magazine, the right to sell it to other United States or foreign magazines to publish, the right to sell it to the movies, and, in short, the right to sell and make money on that story in any way whatever and in as many ways as possible.

It does not make any difference, incidentally, if you sell the story under a pen name without revealing that it is not your real name, get the check issued to you under the pen name, and sign and manage to cash it under the false name. Under law, the publisher has paid for the story and all its rights in full and in good faith, and you have consummated the deal and accepted the payment in full by endorsing the check, whatever the name you have used and signed. The publisher, therefore, still owns the story, and completely.

More than 70 per cent of all magazine publishers today purchase all rights when they accept the story, either with a one-line notice as described or with a longer notice which lists and details each of the rights they are getting, and will usually pass up a story rather than alter their regular purchase arrangements in any way. Actually, however, this is not as bad as it sounds.

In the earlier days of magazine publishing, most publishers who bought all rights did so with the attitude that they wanted to make as much money as possible out of the story—and to hell with the author. There is still some of that sort of thing in the publishing field, of course, but the long fight against this practice on the part of agents and writers' organizations, plus the entry into the business of many more fair-minded publishers, has brought it down to a minimum. Today most publishers who buy all rights do so to protect themselves against competitive appearances of the story, particularly around the same period in which *they* publish it, and will usually release all unused rights back to the author upon request directly or a few months after publication. Nearly all do so gratis; a very few request a small percentage of the earnings, if any, from sale of remaining rights.

Some other publishers do not ask for all rights, but instead purchase "all serial rights," and I'd better explain this because the word "serial" is a little misleading when used in connection with rights. It does not refer, as you might think, only to long stories which are broken up and published in several issues in episode form; it refers to the publication of a story of any kind in a periodical, magazine, or newspaper, either in one complete installment or many. Serial rights, in other words, are the rights which permit publication of material in periodicals, as differentiated, for example, from the rights which permit publication of material in book form, which are, of course, book rights.

The serial rights inherent in a story are divisible in two ways: by countries or groups of countries, and by the chronology of appearances of the story in periodicals in those countries or groups of countries. To put it another way, a story, provided each purchasing publisher buys only the right to publish it once in his periodical and nothing more, may sell to many periodicals in each country or group of countries, and then start all over again in each new country or group of countries and do the same thing. The first publisher who runs a story in a country or group of countries buys and uses up first serial rights for that territory, which is the premium right because it means that the readers of his periodical will be getting a story brand-new to that territory; all subsequent periodicals which run the story in that territory buy and use second serial rights for the territory. The territory is determined by the country or countries covered by the circulation of the publishing magazines.

To give an example, let us say that you write a story and sell it to a magazine which circulates only in the United States. The publication of the story by this magazine uses up "first United States serial rights," since, as I have said, first serial rights exist only once in each territory. Subsequently, a magazine devoted to republishing classics or very good previously published stories wants to use your story, and that magazine only circulates in the United States; the right you sell them which permits them to do so is "second United States serial rights." Unlike first serial rights, which are gone after first publication of a story in a territory, second serial rights are inexhaustible; the term refers to all periodical publication of the story after the initial publication. Therefore, you may later again sell "second United States serial rights" to another magazine which specializes in republishing famous stories, and again to a newspaper syndicate which specializes in using reprint stories, and so on.

You have only, thus far, dealt with United States markets. You can, therefore, move your rights on the story to Canadian markets; and sell "first Canadian serial rights" to a Canadian magazine which circulates only in Canada, and sell subsequent "second Canadian serial rights" in the same way as you have in the United States. And the same principle, of course, applies throughout the world: if your story is sufficiently outstanding to make the grade in various countries, you can sell first, and then second, Australian serial rights; first, and then second, Norwegian serial rights, and on down the line. In foreign-language countries, the purchasing publisher handles the translation.

If your initial magazine purchaser, of course, circulates his periodical throughout North America, as is often the case, he will have to purchase, even if he is interested only in getting the necessary rights and nothing more, "first North American serial rights," which means, naturally, that you cannot again sell first serial rights in any North American country. Where a magazine circulates in the United States, its territories and possessions, and Canada, "first serial rights in the United States, its territories and possessions, and Canada" would have to be bought and used; where a publisher puts out a foreign edition of his magazine, for example, in England, in addition to covering the United States and Canada with his regular edition, he will have to buy at least "first serial rights in the United States, Canada, and England," or "first serial rights in the United States and Canada, and the right to publish in the English edition," which means the same thing. You are then, of course, restrained from selling first serial rights to other periodicals in those countries, though you do have second serial rights left.

The firms which buy second serial rights, incidentally, are not to be confused with old-time magazine reprint publishers. The periodicals which buy second serial rights are those whose purpose is largely that of acting as anthologies; such as digest magazines, or those to whom the provision of fiction or general articles is an added attraction rather than the primary purpose, and don't care particularly whether or not the yarns they publish are appearing for the first time, such as newspaper supplements. These firms pay, of course, for their use of the previously published material, and make no pretense or deception that the material is brand-new. Magazine reprint publishers of the old school are those who used to buy all rights to a brand-new story so that they would own it outright, publish the yarn, wait a few years, and then publish it again as a new story with the title changed and with the names of the lead characters altered. Obviously this stunt is unfair: to the reader because it dupes him into buying a magazine which he believes contains all new stories instead of some he may already have read, and to the author because it cuts down his markets and makes his old stories (for which he receives no further payment) act as competition at those markets to his new ones. The government has pretty much stamped out this practice.

The various nonserial rights—motion picture, radio, television, and so on—may be sold before, simultaneously with, or after the sale of first serial rights in a territory. Generally they are sold afterward, because comparatively few magazine publishers will buy a manuscript when there is a chance that the movie version, or television version, or hard-covered book version, will beat the magazine version in getting out before the public. Some publishers don't care particularly about the nonprint versions such as motion pictures and television, but don't want to have the material come out in book form before they publish it in the magazine, and therefore buy "all publishing rights"—a combination of serial rights and book rights—and return all but the rights they have used once the story is in print. When, however, a nonserial sale and use does precede the serial sale, it does not affect the serial sale in any way: the first appearance of the material in a periodical is still first serial rights, and subsequent appearances in periodicals in the territory are second serial rights.

There is, however, one possible variation in this situation: when a first-serial-rights sale is made on a story either before or after its appearance as a book, and another peridical subsequently buys the story to run in condensed form as a "condensation of the book." Here another right comes to life: "condensation rights," which is a sort of cousin of second serial rights. Like second serial rights, condensation rights can only be sold after a first-serial-rights appearance itself (in the case, for example, where a book is published and then condensed in a magazine without prior periodical publication); and, also like second serial rights, it can be sold again and again within the same territory. Usually, however, each purchaser of condensation rights will request that a specific period of time be allotted before any other periodical is permitted to run a condensation of the book.

Like serial rights, book rights may be sold separately in each country or group of countries, and fall into two categories depending upon order of publication. The initial publication, including all its printings, gives the publisher in each territory book rights, such as "United States book rights," or "United States and Canadian book rights," or "French book rights"; and each subsequent book publication (cheaper editions, dollar editions, paperback editions) give the publisher— whether the same publisher or another firm entirely—"reprint book rights," also often called simply "reprint rights." Television and radio rights can sometimes be sold over and over again to different programs, but the purchase of motion picture rights to a story usually gives the producer exclusive rights to movie versions forevermore.

One other rather common rights occurrence should be mentioned: the fact that some top-level magazine firms purchase all rights at first, and then following their publication do *not* give back all rights other than those they've used— but instead give back only all nonserial rights and all serial rights outside their territory, and keep all serial rights *within* their territory permanently. The reason they first purchase all rights, as stated, is that they pay enough money for their stories so that they want to run them first without being beaten by any version whatsoever (even a very different kind of version like a television dramatization); and the reason they keep all serial rights in their territory permanently is that they feel that any periodical published in the same territory is in a sense competitive to them. They protect against giving these competitors aid and comfort, therefore, by giving back only all nonserial rights and all serial rights *outside* their territory, but hang onto the remaining serial rights within their territory so that no other periodical in their territory will ever republish a story which *they* discovered and bought and published originally.

Here is the most valuable piece of advice anyone can ever give you on the matter of complex contracts: don't try to figure them out for yourself. If you have an agent, he will explain the details of your contracts to you, and see that you get good ones; but if you don't have an agent, go to a good lawyer. Most publishing contracts today are honest and aboveboard, but the legal mind sees things a bit differently from the lay mind, and you may find yourself in trouble or disappointed if you misunderstand or misinterpret some of the clauses.

The best attorney for advice on involved contracts—and on all other publishing problems, for that matter—is one who specializes in publishing affairs. If you live in or around New York City, the local office of the Bar Association will recommend several. If you don't, see a general practitioner—but in that case, go for interpretation rather than advice. There are too many angles and special aspects in the writing business which a man outside it may not know or consider. Just get the attorney to explain each clause in simple, nonlegal language and, by measuring these against the yardstick of your own experience in the writing business, decide for yourself whether or not the contract is fair.

31

ANOTHER HORIZON: *Article writing*

A great many fiction writers do occasional articles for extra money until they hit the Big Time, and even afterward, when an exceptionally good article possibility comes along. You may want to do the same thing yourself, so let's have a look at this article field.

Rates for articles start from about $15 per at the little markets to $750 and up at the big ones; check your market lists for rates of specific magazines. There are three general types which sell today: the opinion article; the educational-helpful article, and the amusement-entertainment article. We'll examine each kind in turn.

The opinion article is exactly what it sounds like: one man's personal ideas and views on a subject. Into this class would go such articles as *What We Must Do About the Southern Problem, Why We'll Never Travel to Other Planets,* and others along the same lines.

The important thing to remember about the opinion article is that the views and ideas expressed therein must be backed up by special authority on the subject. Once in a very great while, a magazine will receive an especially perceptive and original-thinking article from a non-authority, and will buy and run it—usually with a title which points up the writer's lack of special authority (such as *A Housewife Looks at State Government,* or *A Taxpayer Surveys the New Tax Laws*) plus a blurb which states proudly that "everyday people" can do sensible thinking on the popular topics and quarrels of the day, too. These articles are run for variety and are the rare exceptions to the rule: the other nine hundred and ninety-nine thousand, nine hundred and ninety-seven of each million opinion articles by everyday people get the quick heave-ho into the rejection stack.

The editor realizes, in a nutshell, that today's facilities for mass dissemination of information have made the average reader pretty perceptive and knowledgeable himself on popular or controversial topics, and that the reader doesn't particularly care to hear opinions on the subjects from people like himself who have gotten the information in the same way he has—through newspapers, radio and television, other magazine articles, and the like. He wants articles from people on the inside, people with special or additional knowledge—in other words, from recognized authorities on the subject.

It's pretty foolish, and almost always a waste of valuable writing time, to do opinion articles under your own by-line if you are not a recognized authority on some important or interesting subject. The way the non-authority professional writer fits into the opinion-article picture is by doing the article for the authority—either under the authority's lone by-line or under a dual, as-told-to by-line (for example, *Why Monkeys Will Never Replace Man,* by John C. Anthropologist, as told to Amanda Author).

Your initial impression may be that this leaves you out if you don't know any authorities or live in a small town, but, actually, that isn't the case. One of our clients, for instance, specializes in opinion articles by authorities and earns $25,000 a year writing them, despite the fact that he lives in a small Midwestern town and did not know a single authority personally when he started out. He arranged with a reporter on a newspaper in the nearest large town to tip him off (for a small sum per tip) when a nationally famous figure arrived for a brief stay—a well-known political figure, or a millionaire tycoon, or a famous figure in sports or motion pictures. When someone who interested him turned up, he sat down and thought of a good controversial topic in line with the authority's profession on which he would very likely be interested in expressing an opinion. And then he phoned the celebrity or his secretary and said that he wanted to work with the authority on an article on the subject, stressing heavily the good or pleasant publicity which would result from publication of the article. In almost every case, particularly after he'd already sold a few and could name the magazines in which he'd appeared and the celebrities with whom he'd worked, he was told to come up and discuss it—and he almost always came out with permission to do the article.

As in everything else in life, the toughest time for the would-be opinion article writer is the breaking-in period: because many well-known people are unwilling to waste time or work with an unestablished author. Some celebrities are even unwilling to work with established free-lance writers: they'll work only with actual staff-writer employees of magazines. Your best fight against this is a sincere and strong sales talk: to the effect that your discussion with them won't take too long, that at worst they'll only waste a little time and at best gain valuable publicity and space in a national magazine, and that you're trying to break in and make a living, and how about a break? It will often do the trick.

Once you get your opinion article, or while the matter is still in the negotiation stage, the question of division of payment will come up. Most writers who do opinion articles regularly won't share their sales check with the authority at all; they'll drop the project entirely if the authority insists on getting a cut. The Midwestern writer I've mentioned has never yet shared a check with an authority, and he says he never will: his stand on the matter, and one which he expresses frankly to the authority, is that the earnings from opinion articles and other writings are his livelihood, while a share to the authority is just "extra money" and frequently not really needed at all. Then he stresses again the fact that sale and publication of the article gives the authority good national publicity, which should be reward enough.

Remember that the article will appear as though the authority had written it, with his by-line the sole or important one. Don't ever misquote him, or include opinions of your own which happen to disagree with his. For one thing, most authorities will insist on approving the text of an article before it is sent to market, and most editors will require an expression of the authority's approval in writing before they will run the piece. And even when neither insists and the misquoted piece gets into print, word will get around and you'll have a hard time getting other authorities to co-operate on future material.

The educational-helpful article is also exactly what its name says: it is the article which helps while it educates. It is the personal application piece, the article with "you" appeal.

Typical educational-helpful articles are the profit-by-my-experience-and-do-this-or-don't-do-that type (for example, *How I Made My Stepchild Love Me, How I Regained My Son's Respect, I Was an Alcoholic,* etc.), which are, in a way, opinion pieces backed with the authority of personal experience; the everyday psychology type (such as *Don't Pamper Your Children* or *How to Conquer Fear of Heights*), though you'd better make *these* recognized-authority's-opinion pieces and get a doctor, nurse, or psychologist to sign them if you go deeper than common sense and logic and into technical psychology; useful information pieces (such as *How to Make Money from Old Photographs* and *How to Build Lamps from Old Bottles*); and pieces which give news of *personal* importance to the reader and his way of life (for example, *Will a New Discovery Eliminate Tooth Decay?* or *How One Town Licked Racial Prejudice*).

Don't, incidentally, confuse the education-helpful article with the stright educational article, which few editors buy. At one time, many magazines ran straight educational articles (for example, *How Our Flag Was Born* or *How Silkworms Create Silk*); today (outside of the juvenile magazines, where education is a primary purpose) most editors feel that that sort of thing belongs more properly in an encyclopedia—because it has neither sufficient entertainment value nor sufficient personal application value to fit the grip-the-reader requirements of magazine material. Just keep in mind both halves of the educational-helpful classification, and you won't go wrong.

The greatest pitfall in the educational-helpful article is triteness. Try to choose subjects on which you can present advice or information which have not been given before to the average reader, or at least not too often before. And be sure to choose subjects which will interest the bulk of the audience, rather than just a few members. Most people, for example, are interested in new advances in polio and cancer cure, because these are things which may affect them personally, or may affect people who are close to them. It is doubtful, however, that you can sell a general magazine an article on advances in the study of Huntington's chorea, one of the rarest diseases in the world.

The remaining category, the amusement-entertainment article, covers the fact piece whose sole purpose is to divert the reader by telling him about someone or something interesting and unusual. It includes profiles and personality sketches of colorful and famous people (movie stars, politicos, business magnates, and so on); articles about people who have very unusual occupations (such as a professional dog walker, or a woman whose sole job is thinking up screwy stunts for people to try on a television audience-participation show); articles about people who do unusual things (such as a man who builds beautiful miniature houses out of matchsticks,

or a man who spends his time debunking proverbs and popular sayings by selling iceboxes to Eskimos and the like); articles about unusual events (such as a day when red rain fell,
or the time a detective set out to catch a mass murderer and
discovered he had been doing the killings himself while sleep-
walking); articles about unusual places (such as a school for
auctioneers, a museum of horrors, or a church with a huge altar
made of pure gold); and so on.

The important aspect of the amusement-entertainment article, and the factor which usually determines its salability or
lack of salability, is whether or not its subject is sufficiently
unusual and interesting to grip the reader—or, more properly,
the varied readers who made up the typical general magazine
audience.

Let us say, for example, that you do an article about a
woman in your home state who started out with some ideas
about millinery but almost no money—and in five years built
herself a millinery business which brings her a personal income of about $20,000 a year. The story of the woman and
her success is interesting, but probably not interesting enough
to make the article salable because a great many other people
have built similar successes in about the same amount of time
and degree. On the other hand, however, a man who built a
multimillion-dollar corporation in a short time and with very
little money would make an excellent article subject—because
his story is sufficiently unusual to grip *any* reader's attention.

The same thing would apply, as another example, to a
travel article. If you write a piece about your recent trip to
Mexico City, where you went to all the points of interest as
recommended by the travel agency, your article will have a
hard time selling because there's nothing particularly interesting or unusual about it. If, however, you ran into an unusual
experience there—you came upon a strange tribe of people in
one of the isolated sections, people who could leap twenty-
five feet into the air—and you can document this fact to the

editor's satisfaction, you've got yourself an amusement-entertainment article which will sell like a shot.

The fact that something is interesting to you and your friends, or to the people in your home area, will not necessarily mean that that something is a suitable subject for a salable article. It must be measured against the yardstick of the entire country, and all the different kinds of people in it. If the subject would really be interesting and unusual to everybody, and hasn't already been heavily covered, it should be okay.

Many good markets almost never use photos to illustrate the articles they publish, and a few of the very big ones have to secure pix for the articles they buy. A lot of other magazines, however, use photographs and have no facilities for sending their own photographers, and prefer that the writer supply them. It is a good idea, therefore, to provide photos—or at least the promise of them—whenever possible with the amusement-entertainment articles you submit.

Sometimes you can get good photos right from the subject (for example, from the man himself if you're doing a personality piece, or from the business owner or his public relations department if you're doing an article about an unusual or interesting enterprise, or from the Chamber of Commerce or equivalent if you're doing an article about an unusual town or point of interest); sometimes you can buy appropriate photographs cheaply from national photo agencies or from local newspaper offices; sometimes it is necessary to take pictures. Some writers buy a few books on photography and a camera and learn to take pix themselves whenever necessary; others make arrangements with steady photographer collaborators, or with local photographers, and split editorial checks with them—or, since most magazines pay extra for photos used (around $5 to $10 per black-and-white, $25 and up for color), pay them with the extra photo money. Don't however, go out on a limb and take or buy photos when you can do so only at great expense. Just include a note with your article to the effect that photos are available and you'll supply them if the script is okay.

The best way to write an article of any kind is in the anecdotal manner. Start off with a little dramatic or amusing story which leads into your subject, and go on from there to cover the subject—using as many additional dramatic or amusing anecdotes as possible. You'll find heavy use of the anecdotal article treatment in almost all the general magazines; study the structure carefully. Sometimes—particularly when your article is about a past event—it is preferable to use a dramatic narrative style almost as though you are writing a fiction piece, but in most cases anecdotal handling is best.

At one time, very few article writers would do a complete script before querying five or six likely markets to check editorial reactions to the subject. Today, the reverse is true; the greater number of successful article writers hardly query at all. The reason stems from a simple factor—it is too often difficult, or even impossible, for an editor to get an accurate picture of an article idea's potentialities unless he sees how it is handled in the complete piece. As a result, many writers found that editors would nix idea after idea, and yet buy complete scripts from them which had been built on ideas and subjects which were no better. In the opposite direction, writers found that an editor's go-ahead on an idea was no real guarantee of subsequent purchase of the finished script, either; complete articles based on query okays were bought and rejected in about equal ratio to the complete articles which were sent without previous query. Obviously, an editor makes no commitment when he looks over a brief description of an article idea and replies that it looks interesting and he'd like to see the complete piece; just as obviously, he may be tempted to okay anything which doesn't look downright terrible rather than take the chance of missing out on a good one.

These facts explain why so many article writers work today

in the same way as fiction writers: they write the scripts, and then send them along to logical markets until they sell. The consensus is that the only time a query is necessary is when your subject is so timely and hot that other writers may think of it when you do, and the query is more in the nature of a reservation—so that the editor will be expecting your script and won't buy another on the same subject in the meantime.

From the description of the various types of salable article subjects in the preceding pages, you have probably realized that, as in fiction work, you get article ideas from the things you read, and the things around you, and all the other factors of your own experience.

When you get an idea, you'll know pretty well, from your careful and regular reading of magazines, whether or not the subject has been covered recently, or too often in the past. Make a further check, however; go to your local public library and look up the subject in the various guides to periodical literature. These guides don't list every article published, but they do list every article published in many of the major magazines, and they'll give you a pretty good picture of whether you've hit on something fresh or something which has already been done to death.

32

YOU'RE ON YOUR OWN

In some future superatomic age, perhaps, stories will be written by Authorship Machines, and a writer will be a sort of engineer who brings forth different types of stories on call by pressing different combinations of six or seven buttons. When that is the case, there will probably also be precision instruments to measure the quality and correctness of the problem, complications, language, transitions, and all the other ingredients which make up a work of fiction.

Today, however, a story is strictly a handmade affair, and the manner in which a story is judged is just as informal and unprecise. Few editors, if any, actually sit down and judge a story by each of its separate components; few, if any, actually say to themselves, in as many words, "Is the problem strong enough? Are the complications worrisome enough? Are the descriptions vivid enough? Are the transitions smooth enough?" It is the total effect, the total reaction, given by a story which usually determines its acceptance or rejection.

You will not, as I have said, necessarily have an unsalable script on your hands if some of the ingredients of your story are not so good, or not as good as they might be. Exact perfection is for machines; it is rarely if ever achieved by man. The facts and techniques discussed in this book, however, are the means toward achieving the desirable and necessary satisfying *total* effect in your stories, and I hope that you will consider them carefully and use them wisely.

That about seems to cover it. Good luck: and may all your troubles be little ones, and your sales checks big ones.

INDEX